THE VA...RE
FROM TRAILS TO SUMMITS

Derek A. Wolfe

The Valley of Fire
From Trails to Summits
by Derek A. Wolfe

Cover Photo Credits

Photo by Holly Gilhart Wolfe

Opening Page Photo Credits

Arch Rock, photo by Holly Gilhart Wolfe

Book Credits

Illustrations and maps: Derek A. Wolfe
Editors: Donna Wolfe and Brian Wolfe
Cover design: Derek A. Wolfe & Sarah Nicholson
Layout and book design: Derek A. Wolfe & Sarah Nicholson
All photos by the author, unless otherwise noted.

READ THIS BEFORE USING THIS BOOK:

Photo by Holly Gilhart Wolfe

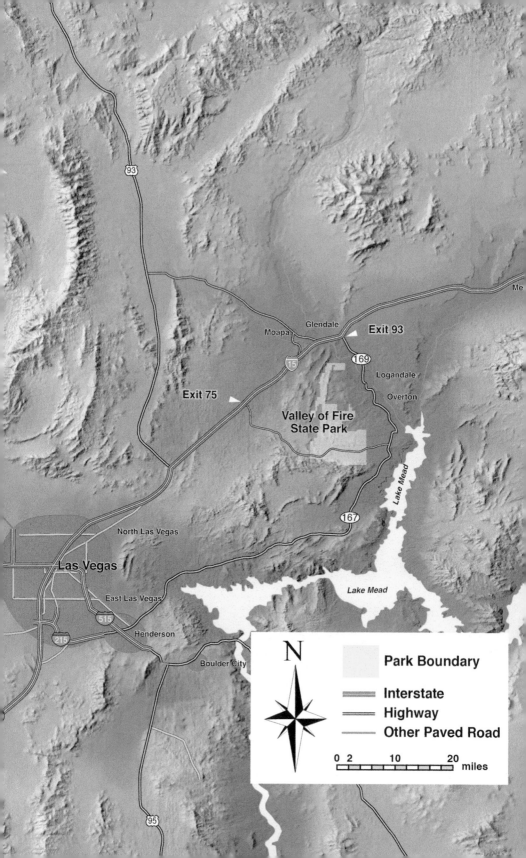

Hiking Trails

Unofficial Trails

Northern Peaks

Southern Peaks

Dangers of the Desert

The desert presents a harsh and unforgiving environment. Extreme weather, strident wildlife and unpleasant plants can turn an enjoyable outing into a nightmare.

Perhaps the greatest hazard in the desert is the extreme weather. Temperatures can easily exceed 110 degrees Fahrenheit in the summer and drop to 20 degrees Fahrenheit in the winter. It is not uncommon to experience 50 degree temperature swings in a day.

Headaches, nausea, dizziness and muscle aches can mark the onset of dehydration, heat exhaustion or heat stroke for the ill prepared. Avoid hiking in the heat of the day. Also, an adequate amount of water should always be carried. It is always better to carry too much water than not have enough. Do not rely on pot-holes or tinajas for safe drinking water.

During monsoon season, mid-July through August, thunderstorms can quickly develop, producing large amounts of precipitation in isolated areas. Lightning can also be of concern if you're on the summit of any peak. Also, it seems every plant in the desert wants to bite. Many plants are ready to leave thorns or needles in an individual's flesh.

The best way to minimize encounters with these hazards is to get properly educated and to enter the desert adequately prepared. As the Boy Scout motto goes, "Be prepared."

Photo by Gerod Green

Rules and Regulations

The desert is extremely fragile. Uneducated, careless and reckless users in the past have left lasting impacts which will take many years to restore to its natural condition. Please remain on trails, in washes or on slickrock whenever possible to help avoid damaging the desert landscape. If you notice a trail has logs or "rock necklaces" blocking it, do not cross the logs or rocks and do not hike on the closed trail.

It is your responsibility to know and obey park regulations and route/trail closures. Please observe these following rules:

- Drive only on approved routes of travel and park only in designated places along the roadside shoulders. Motor vehicles are not allowed on trails. Please observe and obey all posted speed limit signs.

- Camp only in designated campground sites.

- Fires are permitted only in designated grills and fireplaces.

- All plants, animals, artifacts, rocks and minerals are protected by state law. Please do not remove or disturb them.

- Pets are welcome, but they must be kept on a leash of not more than six feet in length. They are not allowed in the visitor center.

- All artifacts and other signs of early civilization and recent history are protected by state and federal law.

- Please conserve the water.

- Use the provided trash containers.

- The park is open from sunrise to sunset unless camping in campgrounds or group camping area. After sunset activity is limited to those areas.

- Rock climbing is limited to specific areas in the park. Inquire at the visitor center.

Minimum Impact

Why write a guide book to lure people to the outdoors only to increase the potential impact or damage? There is no doubt that outdoor recreational sports are increasing in popularity and I am a firm believer that we are going to love our outdoors to death. People are already flocking to the desert in droves and I believe that writing a guide will help establish guidelines and minimize the impact on these peaks and trails to help preserve them for future generations. Perhaps the best way to minimize impacts on the outdoors is to become properly educated and constantly practice minimalist travel techniques. There are several driving forces that entice people to visit the desert and if we do our part, we can ensure everyone can have an enjoyable experience.

Cryptobiotic Soil

Appearing as bulgy black clumps of mud, cryptobiotic soil is everything but a clump of mud. Cryptobiotic soil is a biological crust composed of various living organisms that play an important part of the desert ecosystem. The crust helps prevent soil erosion by wind and water, helps provide organic nutrients to plants and helps absorb and hold water in the arid landscape. Unfortunately, cryptobiotic soil is extremely fragile and can be easily destroyed.

One footstep can ruin decades of growth. When in an area of cryptobiotic soil always think "crypto tip-toe." To help preserve this unique soil, follow these guidelines:

- Watch your step. Be diligent of cryptobiotic soil.

- Stay on established trails. Do not create new trails.

- Hike on slickrock or in sandy washes.

- Hike in single file.

General Minimal Impact Practices

- It is the responsibility of all park visitors to know and obey park regulations and route/trail closures.

- Avoid large groups. If part of a larger group, branch into smaller groups and start an hour apart.

- Respect others and their wilderness experience.

- Pack it in, pack it out. Pack all trash out and dispose of it properly.

- Leave what you find; not limited to plants, rocks, driftwood, antlers or artifacts.

- Always try to leave the environment better than the way you found it. Pack out other peoples' trash.

- Respect plants, natural artifacts and wildlife.

- Keep loud noises to a minimum.

- The desert landscape does not make for good bathrooms. Try to complete any urges before or after your hike. If the urge is irresistible in an undeveloped area, dig a cat-hole 6-8 inches deep at least 200 feet away from water sources and trails. Pack out all toilet paper in ziplock bags. Better yet, use a wag bag.

- Watch your step. Avoid straying off trail and be diligent of cryptobiotic soil. Keep to slickrock and sandy washes when possible.

- Do not climb, scramble or walk upon, wrap webbing or rope around, or rappel off any natural arch.

- Vehicles and bicycles must travel on designated roads and trails.

How to Use This Book

I have spent many days driving, hiking, running and scrambling all over the entire park to provide the best possible information. There is no guarantee that the information contained in this book is accurate or reliable and it may not include all obstacles, trail junctions or hazards encountered. My intent is not to over inflate or "sandbag" any of the ratings. Go prepared.

Hiking Trail Format

Distance – The approximate total round-trip, unless specified one way, hiking distance given in miles. These are estimated distances using a variety of techniques from computer software to GPS.

Elevation Gain – The approximate expected elevation gain in hundreds of feet. These are estimated elevation gains.

Time Required – The time required should only be used for planning purposes and is an estimate to complete the hike from car to car. These times may vary based on conditions, photo stops, group size, getting lost or other unforeseen factors.

Trail Surface – The overall trail surface that is to be expected on the hike.

Rating – Ratings are subjective. For very fit individuals, all of the established trails in the park may seem easy. I've tried to compare the trails to each other and use mileage, elevation gain, obstacles and navigation challenges as a base guideline. Here is the breakdown:

> **Easy –** Less than 2 miles and less than 300 feet gain. The trail is well-established and easy-to-follow. There will be no major navigation issues or obstacles.

> **Moderate –** 2 to 5 miles in length 300 to 700 feet gain. The trail could be hard to follow and some navigation may be required to stay on trail. Obstacles may include short, minor up or down climbs.

> **Difficult -** More than 5 miles and more than 700 feet gain. The trail can be very difficult to follow and navigational skills are required to stay on trail. Expect possible scrambling and tough up or down climbing through sections of trail.

Driving Directions – Using an up-to-date park map in conjunction with these driving directions should help eliminate any excess time driving and searching for trailheads. The most popular trailheads are well signed. If car shuttle parking is an option, these directions will be described in this section. Also, a QR Code is provided which can be used with a smartphone to navigate to the trailhead.

Trail Description – This section will include a general trail description, natural features, trail junctions and obstacles. All "left" and "right" descriptions are from the perspective of looking down-trail. Trails with multiple trailheads are described one way from the most popular trailhead.

Peak Format

Since all of the peaks are off-trail, I've used different guidelines from what I used in the hiking chapters. These peaks should be approached with good judgment, scrambling and off-route navigational experience. Most of the routes are not suitable for casual hikers.

Route Name and Difficulty – This describes the aspect or feature which is used to climb the peak. I've used the YDS (Yosemite Decimal System) class system to describe the difficultly which includes the hardest single move of a route. The class system ranges from 1 to 5.15 while classes 1 to 4 uses a single digit, class 5 breaks down into decimals. Only one scramble in this book ventures into low 5th class territory. Here is the breakdown of class:

> **Class 1** – Hiking on a maintained trail or cross-country terrain that is no harder than a trail. Most established hikes in the park are class 1.

> **Class 2** – Off-trail hiking. This could include rock-hopping, bushwhacking or uneven cross-country hiking. The Prospects Trail has sections of class 2.

> **Class 3** – Easy scrambling. This is the start of climbing and you are no longer using walking motion. The use of your hands are used for upward movement but holds are plentiful. A fall would result in serious injury and could be fatal.

> **Class 4** – Advanced scrambling. Good climbing skills are required since hand and foot placements are searched for, thoughtful and tested. A fall will most likely be fatal.

> **Class 5** – Technical climbing. More advanced climbing movement and technique is required. This includes the use of small foot and handholds, shifting balance and careful evaluation of upward climbing sequences. A rope is usually used.

Distance – This is the approximate total round-trip distance from the trailhead to the summit given in miles.

Elevation Gain – The approximate expected elevation gain in hundreds of feet from the trailhead to the summit along with any elevation gain required back to the trailhead.

Time Required – The time required should only be used for planning purposes and is an estimate to complete a peak from car to car. These times may vary based on conditions, photo stops, group size, getting lost or other unforeseen factors.

Rating – These ratings are my subjective rating regarding the quality of the peak. Four and five star peaks are Valley of Fire classics that should not be missed. Enjoyable, three star peaks are worth climbing but are not as impressive as four or five star peaks. Two star peaks are still worthwhile, but offer nothing memorable or unique to make them stand out.

Route - This section will include a description of the route up the peak. It will describe junctions, features, obstacles and areas of scrambling.

Topo Map – This map will show the route map marked on the USGS quad overlain with satellite imagery along with key GPS waypoints. Although a GPS is not required, they can be helpful in locating parking and identifying important route-finding waypoints. A GPS should always be used in conjunction with a map and compass. All waypoints are in the WGS84 datum and use decimal degrees. Be sure your GPS matches the datum and coordinate type.

It should be noted that the USGS quads for The Valley of Fire show elevations in meters and not feet. Contours are in intervals of 10 meters (32 feet). Also, any yellow arrows displayed on the map will indicate direction of travel.

Chapter 1

Hiking Trails

The Fire Wave. Photo by Bob Biddix

Introduction to Hiking Trails

Valley of Fire offers over 30 miles of spectacular scenic trails. Spend some time to explore and treasure this special place. An enjoyable outing should keep many factors in mind which includes a good assessment of ability, weak members, time, experience, children, weather and fitness. Summers can be astonishingly hot so make sure to go prepared with plenty of water.

The Slot Canyon on the White Domes Loop

Hiking Trails Overview Map

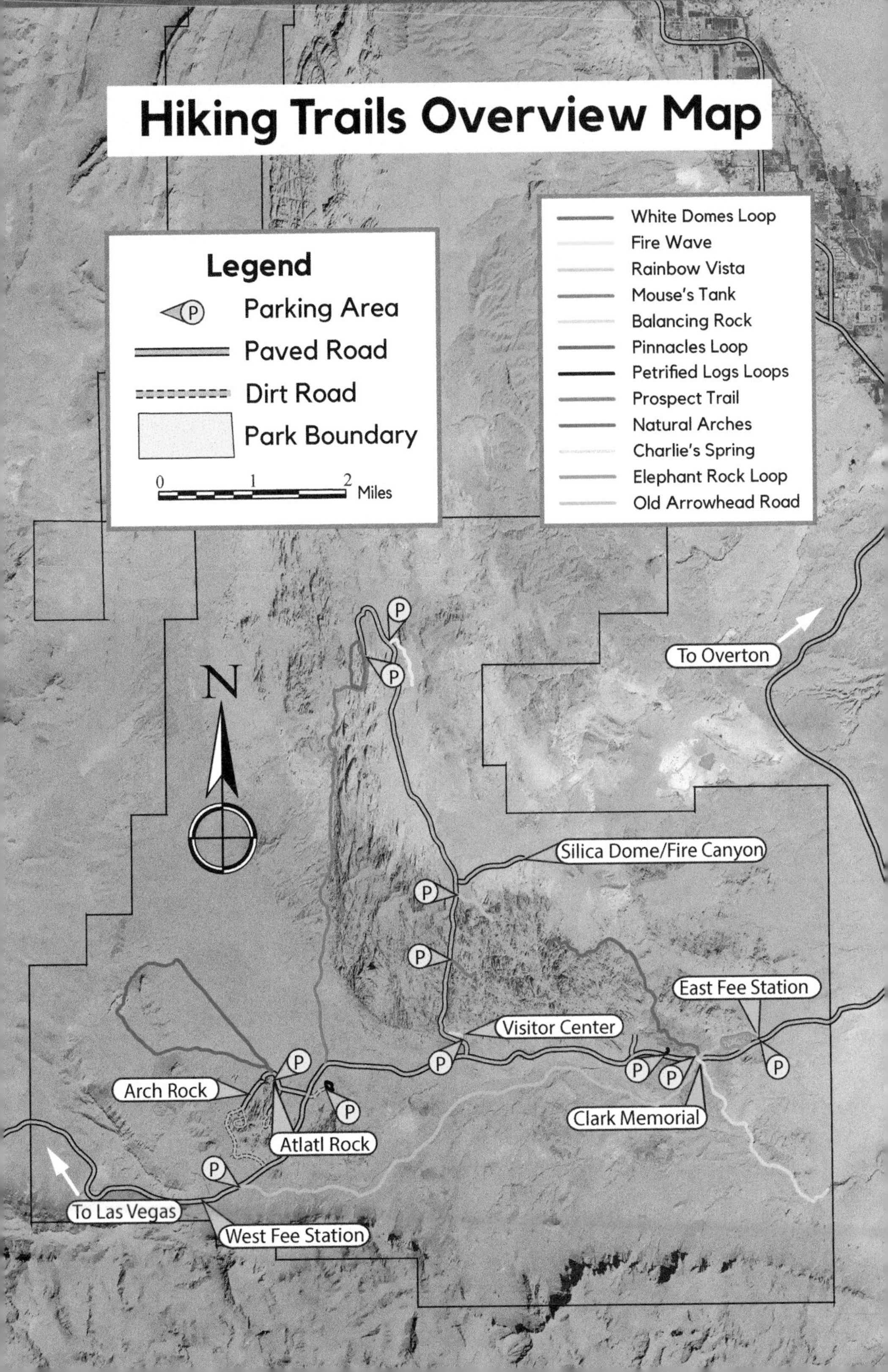

Legend

- ◁Ⓟ Parking Area
- ═══ Paved Road
- ┅┅┅ Dirt Road
- ▭ Park Boundary

0 ——— 1 ——— 2 Miles

Trail Legend
White Domes Loop
Fire Wave
Rainbow Vista
Mouse's Tank
Balancing Rock
Pinnacles Loop
Petrified Logs Loops
Prospect Trail
Natural Arches
Charlie's Spring
Elephant Rock Loop
Old Arrowhead Road

N

To Overton

Silica Dome/Fire Canyon

Visitor Center

East Fee Station

Arch Rock

Atlatl Rock

Clark Memorial

To Las Vegas

West Fee Station

WHITE DOMES LOOP

Distance: ~1.1 Miles
Elevation Gain: ~300 Feet
Rating: Easy

Time Required: 30 Minutes-1.5 Hours
Trail Surface: Sand/Compact Soil

Driving Directions

From the beginning of the White Domes Loop road, drive 5.7 miles north to the well marked White Domes Loop trailhead. This is the end of the road.

Trail Description

With vibrant contrasting colors of white, orange and red, the White Domes Loop trail is one of the most popular trails in the park, well-established and easy to follow.

The trail is normally completed clockwise. Starting from the White Domes parking area, start hiking south up a small sandy hill trail between two striking sandstone domes. The trail then descends down to a bench where an old movie set for the 1966 western movie *The Professionals* was filmed. Continue down trail into a wash as it turns right into a slot canyon. The rising sandstone walls between the sandstone domes is striking.

Once through the short slot canyon, take another right and continue up a hill to a widening vista. The trail then loops back around through more sandstone features depositing you near the rear of the parking area.

FIRE WAVE

Distance: ~1.4 Miles
Elevation Gain: ~250 Feet
Rating: Easy

Time Required: 1-2 Hours
Trail Surface: Sand/Rock

Driving Directions

From the beginning of the White Domes Loop road, drive 4.8 miles north to the well marked Fire Wave trailhead on the left.

Trail Description

The Fire Wave is one of the Park's most photogenic features which consequently makes it one of the most popular hikes. From the parking area, begin hiking down the sandy trail as it traverses around a massive sandstone buttress, Gibraltar Rock. After 0.4 mile, there will be a faint trail junction, stay right on the marked trail.

Continuing down a sandy wash, the trail eventually intercepts colorfully featured slickrock. Follow the slickrock up as it descends down a hill ending at the Fire Wave rock feature. The stratified, multi-colored sandstone is captivating.

White Domes Loop & The Fire Wave Map

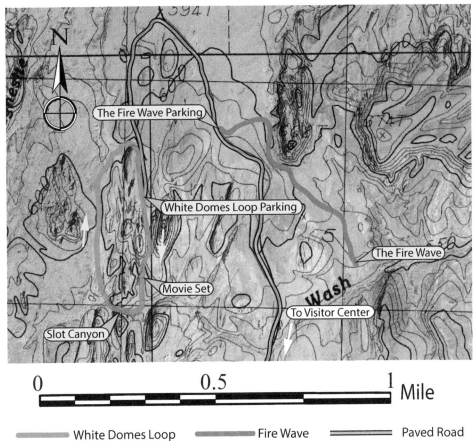

The Fire Wave Parking

White Domes Loop Parking

The Fire Wave

Movie Set

To Visitor Center

Wash

Slot Canyon

0   0.5   1 Mile

White Domes Loop   Fire Wave   Paved Road

Photo by Holly Gilhart Wolfe

RAINBOW VISTA

Distance: ~1.1 Miles   **Time Required:** 30-45 Minutes
Elevation Gain: ~150 Feet   **Trail Surface:** Sand
Rating: Easy

Driving Directions

From the beginning of the White Domes Loop road, drive 1.9 miles north to the well marked Rainbow Vista trailhead.

Trail Description

This short hike leads to a magnificent perch that overlooks Fire Canyon which has mind-blowing landscapes. Moreover, this trail is one of the more popular hikes in the park.

From the Rainbow Vista parking area, start hiking east along a sandy trail which crosses an open valley. Continue following the trail as it transitions into a sandy wash. One minor downclimb will be encountered which can easily be overcome. Shortly after the downclimb, a precipitous drop-off marks the end of the trail. The vibrant red sandstone landscapes overlooking Fire Canyon makes for an excellent position for photos.

Rainbow Vista Overlook

Rainbow Vista Map

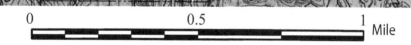

Rainbow Vista Parking

Fire Canyon/Silica Dome Road

White Domes Road

Overlook

To Visitor Center

R K

N

0   0.5   1 Mile

Paved Road

Photo by Holly Gilhart Wolfe

Mouse's Tank
Photo by Holly Gilhart Wolfe

MOUSE'S TANK

Distance: ~0.7 Mile   **Time Required:** 20-40 Minutes
Elevation Gain: ~100 Feet   **Trail Surface:** Sand
Rating: Easy

Driving Directions

From the beginning of the White Domes Loop road, drive 1.2 miles north and make a right turn to the well marked Mouse's Tank trailhead.

Trail Description

Making for a short out and back, this is an excellent excursion for all levels of hikers. It is also one of the most popular hikes in the park. Mouse's Tank is a tinaja, a natural basin for water collection, which was named after an outlaw who used the area as a hideout in the late 1800s.

The trail starts on the east side of the parking area down a sidewalk which quickly ends in a sandy wash. An easy, short sandy hike down-canyon takes you to Mouse's Tank. Keep your eyes open as there are numerous petroglyphs along the trail. Please only take photos of the petroglyphs and do not touch, vandalize or carve your name next to these federally protected antiquities.

Mouse's Tank Map

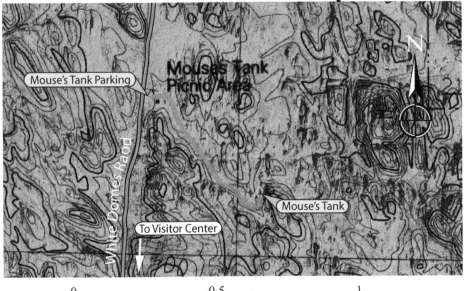

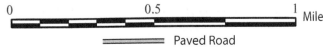
Paved Road

BALANCING ROCK

Distance: ~0.25 Mile   **Time Required:** 10-20 Minutes
Elevation Gain: ~50 Feet   **Trail Surface:** Packed Gravel
Rating: Very Easy

Driving Directions

From the beginning of the White Domes Loop road, drive 0.2 mile north to the Park's Visitor Center.

Trail Description

Arguably this is the easiest hike in the park which takes you to a fantastic rock tower with a precariously perched, balanced rock.

From the visitor center parking area, find the start of the trail on the western edge of the parking lot. If you're starting from the overflow parking area, take a set of stairs toward the visitor center and look for the start of the trail on your left. The trail descends down a small hill and then becomes level which then takes you to the rock formation. There is excellent lighting for photos in both the morning or evening hours.

Balancing Rock Map

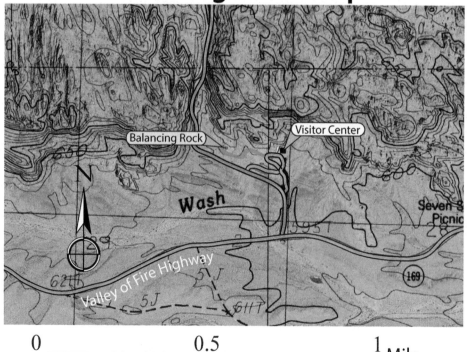

0   0.5   1 Mile

══════ Paved Road

Balancing Rock

PINNACLES LOOP

Distance: ~4.8 Miles
Elevation Gain: ~500 Feet
Rating: Moderate

Time Required: 2.5-4 Hours
Trail Surface: Sand/Soil

Driving Directions

Drive 1.8 miles east on the Valley of Fire highway from the west entrance fee station and turn left on a paved road for Atlatl Rock and The Scenic Loop. If you're driving from the eastern entrance, drive 5.2 miles west from the fee station and turn right onto the road. Continue 0.5 mile on the Scenic Loop and make a left to the Atlatl Rock picnic area parking.

Trail Description

Despite the somewhat longer, unappealing sandy wash approach, this is one of my favorite established hikes in the park as red sandstone towers stretch to the sky in a secluded area. If you are looking to avoid crowds, this is a great alternative.

This loop is best completed clockwise. The trailhead can be somewhat hard to locate. From the Atlatl Rock parking area, cross the Scenic Loop road and look for a trailhead marker directly across from the entry road to the parking lot. This is the trailhead. After 50 yards, the trail quickly deposits you into a wash where you will begin hiking west, northwest.

Hike up the wash, acceptably marked, as the nearby red rock formations of the scenic loop become distant. After 1.4 miles, as the trail makes a turn to the northwest, the Pinnacles unexpectedly come into view. Spend some time at the Pinnacles and enjoy these amazing rock features.

The trail continues north through the Pinnacles where some minor up-climbing is required to reach the top of a hill behind the rock formations. Continue to follow the trail, north, back down a hill as it begins to follow another wash. This wash circles back around Gregg Peak and trends east. After 3.1 miles, keep an eye out for the trail as it exits the wash. You don't want to miss this junction.

Once you have exited the wash, an open desert hike southeast will lead you back to the trailhead. At times, the trail on this portion of the hike can be difficult to follow. Sparsely spaced trail markers reassure you that you're on track.

Pinnacles Loop Map

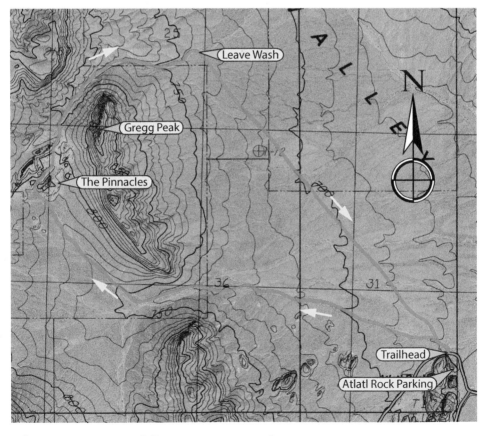

PETRIFIED LOGS TRAILS

Distance: ~0.3 Mile and ~0.1 Mile | **Time Required:** 10-20 Minutes
Elevation Gain: ~50 Feet | **Trail Surface:** Compact Soil
Rating: Very Easy

Driving Directions

Western Loop:
Drive 1.8 miles east on the Valley of Fire highway from the west entrance fee station and turn right on the Petrified Logs Loop road (dirt). If you're driving from the eastern entrance, drive 5.2 miles west from the fee station and turn left onto the Petrified Logs Loop road. Continue an additional 0.2 mile to the trailhead and parking area.

Eastern Trail:
Drive 5.9 miles east on the Valley of Fire highway from the west entrance fee station and if you're driving from the eastern entrance, drive 1.1 miles west from the fee station. A small gravel pullout is located on the north side of the road which serves as the trailhead.

Trail Description

The park is home to two separate petrified log trails. These logs were once part of a primitive evergreen forest made of Araucarian Pines. Surprisingly, these trees are still found in the southern hemisphere.

The western loop is the longer of the two petrified log hikes, has more examples of these fossils and can be completed clockwise or counterclockwise. From the parking area, walk the easy-to-follow loop around a few fenced off areas of petrified logs.

The eastern trail is a short out and back and has only one example of a petrified log. From the parking area, a well maintained packed trail leads up a few stairs to the fossil.

Petrified Logs Trail Maps

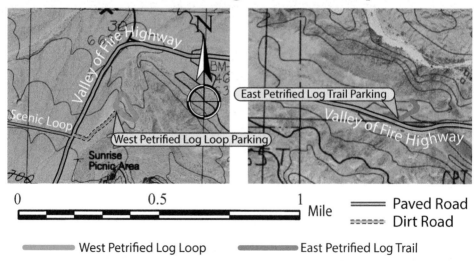

ATLATL ROCK

Distance: ~0.1 Mile | **Time Required:** 10-20 Minutes
Elevation Gain: ~50 Feet | **Trail Surface:** Metal/Concrete
Rating: Very Easy

Driving Directions

Drive 1.8 miles east on the Valley of Fire highway from the west entrance fee station and turn left on a paved road for Atlatl Rock and The Scenic Loop and if you're driving from the eastern entrance, drive 5.2 miles west from the fee station and turn right onto the road. Continue 0.5 mile on the Scenic Loop and make a left to the Atlatl Rock picnic area parking.

Trail Description

Atlatl Rock contains the finest examples of ancient petroglyphs in the park. Preceding the bow and arrow, an atlatl is a throwing stick. Help preserve these artifacts and please only take photos of the petroglyphs and do not touch, vandalize or carve your name next to the petroglyphs. From the parking lot, follow the obvious trail to a metal staircase leading up to the petroglyphs.

Photo by Holly Gilhart Wolfe

PROSPECT TRAIL

Distance: ~4.8 Miles (one way)   **Time Required:** 2-5 Hours
Elevation Gain: North to South   **Trail Surface:** Sand/Compact Soil/
900 Feet, South to North 600 Feet   Rock
Rating: Moderate to Difficult

Driving Directions

Northern Trailhead:
The northern trail is the White Domes Loop trailhead. From the beginning of
the White Domes Loop road, drive 5.7 miles north to the well marked trailhead. This is the end of the road.

Southern Trailhead and Optional Car Shuttle Parking:
Drive 2.2 miles east on the Valley of Fire highway from the western entrance
fee station and turn left at a pullout for the southern Prospect Trail trailhead.
If you're driving from the eastern entrance, drive 4.8 miles west from the fee
station and turn right into the parking area.

Trail Description

This scenic trail offers a variety of sweeping vistas accompanied with some challenging hiking
terrain. Although long, this can be completed as an out and back, or with a car shuttle. Usually people complete this trail from north to south starting at the White Domes Loop parking
area.

Starting from the White Domes parking area, follow the White Domes Loop clockwise by
hiking south up a small sandy hill between two striking sandstone domes. Descend down
the hill, passing *The Professionals* movie set to a wash. Follow the wash up stream, as it turns
right into a slot canyon.

Once through the short slot canyon, instead of turning right to follow the White Domes Loop,
go left and follow the wash as it continues up beautifully sculpted narrows. After the narrows,
the trail heads south up a sandy wash. After 1.3 miles, a tough dryfall is bypassed via a trail on
the left (east) side of the wash. The bypass trail quickly returns back to the main wash. If you're
hiking this trail south to north, this bypass trail can be tricky to identify.

A wonderful red rock buttress lines the horizon as you continue to the south. Before the end
of the wash, there are several small sections of easy scrambles some of which have bypass
trails on the right (west) side of the wash. The trail then leaves the main wash and winds its
way up a small tributary wash to an old road where the trail changes character.

The old road then becomes the trail as you continue south up and over a small hill. Again, the
landscape changes as you hike through a scenic area of red rock sculptures and cliffs. Eventually, you hike out of the red rock garden and start a cross-country desert excursion. If you are
doing this hike as an out and back, this is a great spot to turn around.

Descending into the desert flats, the trail then intersects a well maintained gravel service
road for the remaining 0.4 mile to the southern trailhead.

Prospect Trail Map

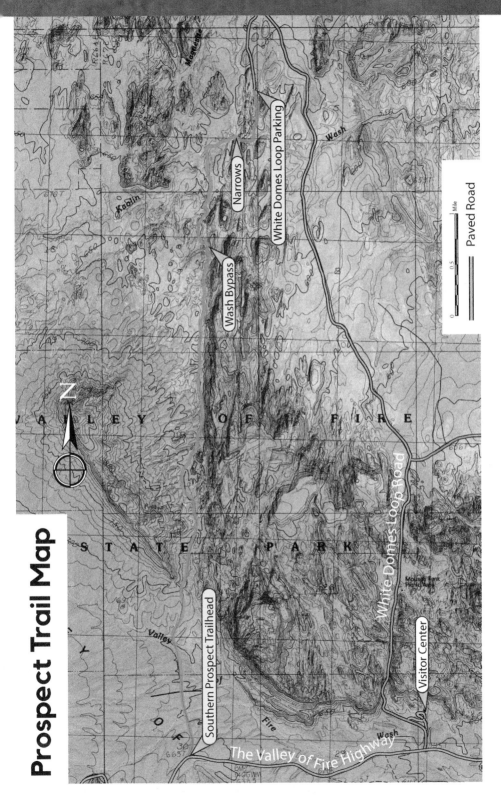

Paved Road

0   0.5   1 Mile

N

VALLEY OF FIRE

STATE PARK

Kaolin

Narrows

Wash Bypass

White Domes Loop Parking

Wash

White Domes Loop Road

Southern Prospect Trailhead

Visitor Center

Mouse's Tank Picnic Area

Valley

Fire

Wash

The Valley of Fire Highway

NATURAL ARCHES

Distance: ~2.5-5.2 Miles
Elevation Gain: ~100-300 Feet
Rating: Moderate

Time Required: 1-4 Hours
Trail Surface: Sand

Driving Directions

Drive 6.3 miles east on the Valley of Fire highway from the west entrance fee station and turn left at a pullout for the trailhead. If you're driving from the eastern entrance, drive 0.7 mile west from the fee station and turn right into the parking area. Do not block access to the service road.

Trail Description

Unfortunately, the most awe-striking arch along this trail collapsed in 2010. Albeit a bit sandy, this hike is still a worthy outing as there are still plenty of arches to find along with exotic rock features and compelling solution pockets. This trail also allows you to explore the fine narrows of Fire Canyon without having to engage in any tough down-climbing or complex dryfall by-passes when completing Fire Canyon from Mouse's Tank.

From the parking area on the north side of the road, follow a trail east that parallels the road 50 yards down to the North Fork of the Valley of Fire Wash; then begin from the parking area on the north side of the road, follow a trail east that parallels the road 50 yards down to Fire Wash; then begin your hike north up Fire Wash. After 0.8 mile, the scenery becomes more interesting as arches and other nifty geological features appear. The trail officially ends after 1.3 miles. Some minor up-climbs will be encountered.

If you continue to follow the wash for an additional 1.3 miles, the red sandstone peaks begin to rise around you and the wash narrows. A beautiful section of narrow canyon will take you to a dryfall that can not be up-climbed. This marks the end of the hike.

Natural Arches Map

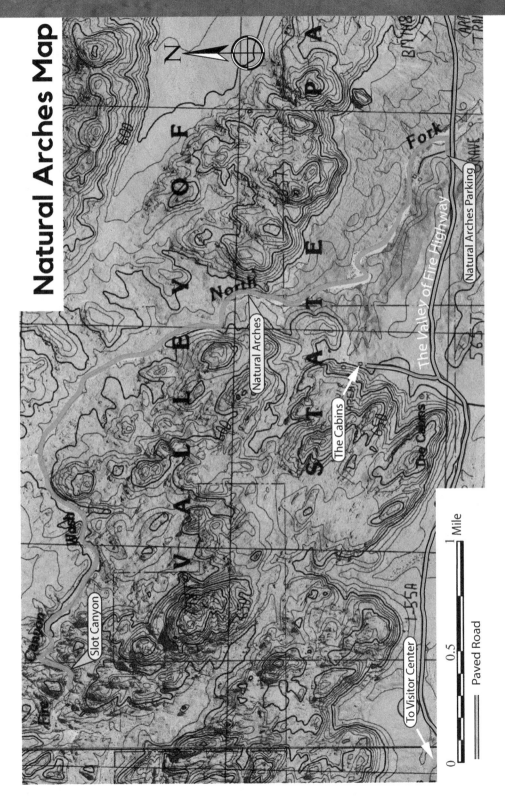

Fork

North

Slot Canyon

Natural Arches

The Cabins

The Cabins

The Valley of Fire Highway

Natural Arches Parking

To Visitor Center

VALLEY OF PA STATE

0   0.5   1 Mile

Paved Road

CHARLIE'S SPRING

Distance: ~4.8 Miles
Elevation Gain: ~300 Feet
Rating: Moderate

Time Required: 2-4 Hours
Trail Surface: Sand

Driving Directions

Drive 6.3 miles east on the Valley of Fire highway from the west entrance fee station and turn left at a pullout for the trailhead. If you're driving from the eastern entrance, drive 0.7 mile west from the fee station and turn right into the parking area. Do not block access to the service road.

Trail Description

This sandy hike leads to the desert oasis of Charlie's Spring which provides year-round water flow. Despite being on the south, less scenic side of the Valley of Fire highway, the views of the Muddy mountains and red rock outcroppings make this hike enjoyable. It's one of the sandiest hikes in the park.

The start of the trail can be difficult to locate. From the parking area, cross to the south side of the Valley of Fire highway and follow the Clark Memorial Trail to the bottom of the wash. Do not head back up a small hill to the Clark Memorial but instead follow a faint trail into the North Fork of the Valley of Fire Wash. This is the start of the trail. At times, the trail can be very sandy and soft; fortunately, the trail slowly transitions from deep sand into gravel. Although the trail isn't marked along the way, it is easy to follow as you stay in the wash the entire time.

Follow Valley of Fire Wash downstream for 2.1 miles where there is an unexpected drop-off into a narrow red sandstone canyon. The drop can easily be conquered with some easy class 2 down-climbing. Hiking in the narrows is an enjoyable change in scenery and provides some of the only shade on the hike. Shortly after the downclimb, the wash becomes lush with vegetation. Some trees and tall grass fill the wash as you arrive at Charlie's Spring.

CLARK MEMORIAL

Distance: ~0.2 Mile
Elevation Gain: ~50 Feet
Rating: Very Easy

Time Required: 15-30 Minutes
Trail Surface: Sand/Compact Soil

Driving Directions

Drive 6.3 miles east on the Valley of Fire highway from the west entrance fee station and turn left at a pullout for the trailhead. If you're driving from the eastern entrance, drive 0.7 mile west from the fee station and turn right into the parking area. Do not block access to the service road.

Trail Description

This quick trail goes to the headstone of John Clark, who served in the Civil War, where his body was found in June 1915. He was traveling to Salt Lake City from Bakersfield and most likely died of dehydration.

From the parking area, cross to the south side of the Valley of Fire highway and follow the Clark Memorial Trail to the bottom of the wash. Then take the trail up a switchback to the top of a petite mesa where Clark's headstone is located.

Charlie's Spring & Clark Memorial Map

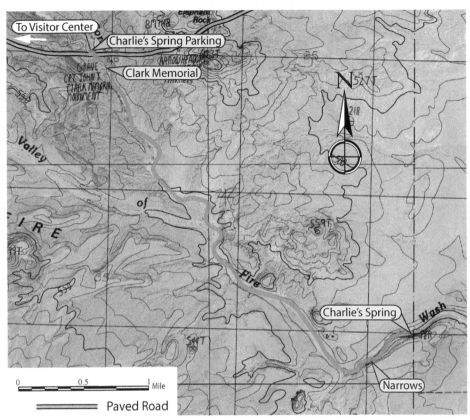

Charlie's Spring

ELEPHANT ROCK LOOP

Distance: ~1.2 Miles
Elevation Gain: ~300 Feet
Rating: Easy

Time Required: 30 Minutes-1 Hour
Trail Surface: Sand/Soil

Driving Directions

This trailhead is located at the eastern fee station which is located 7.0 miles east on the Valley of Fire Highway from the western fee station.

Trail Description

Most folks only complete the short hike from the parking area to Elephant Rock and skip the scenic loop. The loop offers excellent views of the park. There are also several unique rock formations, pockets and arches that can be discovered.

The loop can be hiked clockwise or counterclockwise and starts from the shaded awning on the northwestern edge of the Elephant Rock parking area. The trail is well marked, heavily used and easy to follow. When you arrive at the loop portion of the trail, go left, clockwise to reach Elephant Rock which is at the top of a small hill adjacent to the paved road. Please do not climb on top of Elephant Rock.

If you continue the loop clockwise past Elephant Rock, the trail parallels the Valley of Fire road and descends toward a wash. The views here to the west are excellent. Keep making right turns as the trail snakes its way around a large red sandstone outcropping. As you start heading east on the north end of the loop back toward the parking area, the trail becomes more sandy and has some minor rolling hills.

Elephant Rock Loop

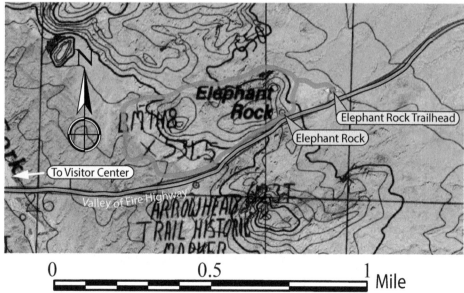

Elephant Rock

OLD ARROWHEAD ROAD

Distance: ~6.9 Miles (one way)
Elevation Gain: East to West 1,100 Feet, West to East 400 Feet
Rating: Moderate to Difficult

Time Required: 2.5-5 Hours
Trail Surface: Sand/Compact Soil/Gravel

Driving Directions

Eastern Trailhead:
This trailhead is located at the eastern fee station which is located 7.0 miles east on the Valley of Fire Highway from the western fee station.

Western Trailhead:
Drive 0.6 mile east on the Valley of Fire highway from the western entrance fee station or if you're driving from the eastern entrance, drive 6.4 miles west from the fee station and use a gravel pullout on the south side of the road. Do not block access to the gravel road.

Drop-in Trailhead:

This trailhead also provides access to the Natural Arches and Charlie's Spring trail. Drive 6.3 miles east on the Valley of Fire highway from the west entrance fee station and turn left at a pullout for the trailhead. If you're driving from the eastern entrance, drive 0.7 mile west from the fee station and turn right into the parking area. Do not block access to the service road.

Trail Description

Between 1914 and 1924, the Arrowhead Trail was utilized as the first all-weather road between Salt Lake City and Los Angeles. The old Arrowhead Road trail follows this historic landmark's path. The trail can be hiked as an out and back or with a car shuttle in either direction. For those seeking shorter hiking options, there is an alternate drop-in trailhead allowing access to a middle section of the trail. This is the only trail in the park that allows horses and bicycles. The trail is well marked but at times, the western portion can be hard to follow.

The easiest way to access the trail is from the Elephant Rock parking area on the east side of the park. Starting from the shaded awning on the northwestern edge of the parking area, follow a well marked trail to a junction. This is the Elephant Rock Loop. Go right at the junction, which follows the Elephant Rock Loop counterclockwise to the southwestern edge of that loop. Keep an eye out for an old road that descends back toward the Valley of Fire Highway. This is the continuation of the Old Arrowhead Road trail.

The old road departs the Elephant Rock Loop trail, descends down a hill and intercepts and parallels the Valley of Fire highway on the north side of the road. The trail then crosses Fire Wash and deposits you at the Natural Arches/Charlie's Spring parking. Cross to the south side of the Valley of Fire highway and look for trail markers that continue south, southwest. The geological character of the trail changes before reaching a wide open desert landscape.

Continuing, the next the 3.5 miles of open terrain offers excellent views of the red rock peaks to the north before wrapping around the south side of Weekapaug Mountain. Once past Weekapaug Mountain, the trail then skirts the south side of the group camping area and Beehives before terminating at the poorly marked western trailhead. If you start from the west, make sure not to hike down the gravel service road which shares the same location as the western trail.

If you're interested in shorter hiking options, park at the Natural Arches/Charlie's Spring trailheads and either proceed east or west on the trail. The western portion of the trail continues on the south side of the Valley of Fire highway while the eastern portion follows a trail to Fire Wash and back up a hill towards the Elephant Rock Loop.

Old Arrowhead Road Map

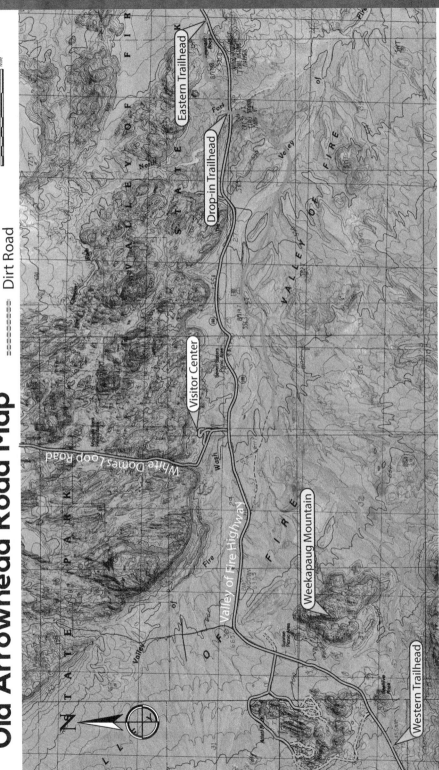

Paved Road
Dirt Road

Eastern Trailhead
Drop-in Trailhead
Visitor Center
Weekapaug Mountain
Western Trailhead

White Domes Loop Road
Valley of Fire Highway

Petroglyphs near Mouse's Tank
Photo by Holly Gilhart Wolfe

Narrows in Fire Canyon

Chapter 2

Introduction to Unofficial Trails

For those seeking more solitude, these trails require more diligence and self reliance. Be prepared for unmarked trails and some additional navigational challenges. Perhaps one of the finest hikes in Valley of Fire is Fire Canyon which offers some of the most scenic areas of narrow canyons in the park.

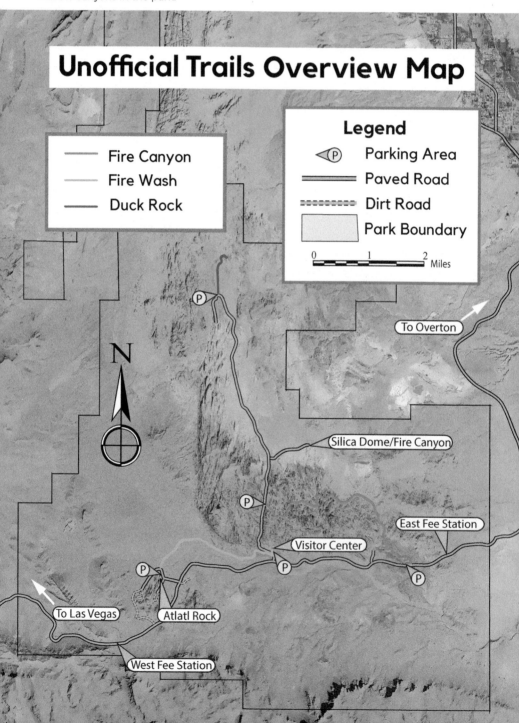

Unofficial Trails Overview Map

Fire Canyon
Fire Wash
Duck Rock

Legend

- ⌐ⓟ Parking Area
- Paved Road
- Dirt Road
- Park Boundary

0 — 1 — 2 Miles

N

To Overton

Silica Dome/Fire Canyon

East Fee Station

Visitor Center

To Las Vegas

Atlatl Rock

West Fee Station

DUCK ROCK

Distance: ~1.8 Miles | **Time Required:** 1-2 Hours
Elevation Gain: ~300 Feet | **Trail Surface:** Packed Gravel/Sand
Rating: Easy

Driving Directions

From the beginning of the White Domes Loop road, drive 5.2 miles north to a pullout for a closed road on the right. This is the most northern curve, before the road turns back south for the White Domes, on the White Domes Loop road.

Trail Description

Marked on older park maps, this was once a popular hike to one of the park's more interesting rock features. Now that the park has closed the road, this is a peaceful hike. Keep in mind this is an unmarked, unmaintained trail. While you're in the area, spend some extra time exploring Magnesite Wash.

From the parking area, start hiking north on a closed road. When reaching the end of the well established road, descend into Magnesite Wash and continue hiking down wash. Once you pass an old, out of place culvert, start looking for Duck Rock on the right. For the best photogenic lighting, complete this hike in late afternoon.

Duck Rock Map

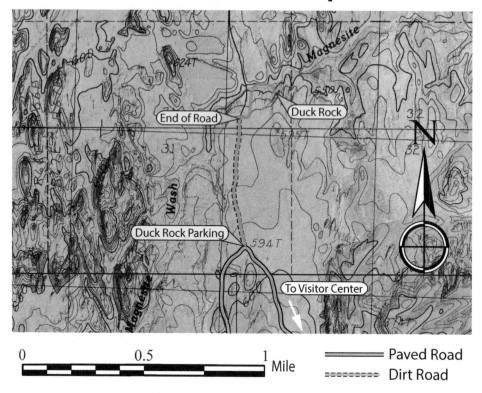

```
0            0.5            1
                              Mile
```

═══════ Paved Road
╌╌╌╌╌╌╌ Dirt Road

VALLEY OF FIRE WASH

Distance: ~2.6 Miles (one way)   **Time Required:** 1-2 Hours
Elevation Gain: West to East 300   **Trail Surface:** Sand/Compact Soil
Feet, East to West 50 Feet
Rating: Easy to Moderate

Driving Directions

West Trailhead:
Drive 1.8 miles east on the Valley of Fire highway from the west entrance fee
station and turn left on a paved road for Atlatl Rock and The Scenic Loop. If
you're driving from the eastern entrance, drive 5.2 miles west from the fee station and turn right onto the road. Continue 0.5 mile on the Scenic Loop and
make a left to the Atlatl Rock picnic area parking.

East Trailhead – Optional Car Shuttle Parking:
From the beginning of the White Domes Loop road, drive 0.2 mile north to
the Park's Visitor Center.

Trail Description

If you're seeking solitude, this trail offers an open desert hike with fantastic views of the Muddy Mountains to the south and red rock summits to the north. This trail is unmarked and can be difficult to follow at times. For the most part, this trail follows an old road and stays out of the wash proper.

From the Atlatl Rock parking area, cross the Scenic Loop road and look for the poorly marked trailhead for the Pinnacles Loop Trail. After 50 yards, the trail quickly deposits you into a wash. Instead of following the Pinnacle Loops trail that stays in the wash heading west, follow an old road north.

After 0.1 mile, the road curves to the northeast. Continue to follow the road as it crosses another wash and after 0.8 mile, the old road will intersect the Prospects Trail and a well maintained gravel service road.

Parallel the service road as the old road continues to head east after the service road ends. The road then intersects a large wash, Valley of Fire Wash, where the trail on the opposite side of the wash can be hard to locate. Continue to follow the old road east as the red rock buttress on your left towers over you. If your route finding is good, you should be able to stay out of the sandy wash entirely by following the old road.

Eventually, the old road will intersect the White Domes Loop road. Turn left and hike north the remaining 0.1 mile to the Visitor Center if you have a car shuttle.

Valley of Fire Wash Map

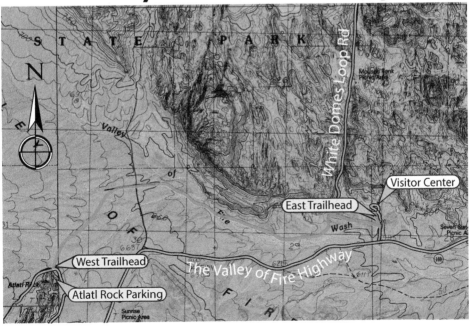

Paved Road

0   0.5   Mile

FIRE CANYON

Distance: ~4.5 Miles (one way) **Time Required:** 3-5 Hours
Elevation Gain: ~100-300 Feet **Trail Surface:** Rock/Sand/Mud
Rating: Very Difficult

Driving Directions

Beginning Trailhead:
From the beginning of the White Domes Loop road, drive 1.2 miles north and make a right turn to the well marked Mouse's Tank trailhead.

Ending Trailhead - Required Car Shuttle Parking:
Drive 6.3 miles east on the Valley of Fire highway from the west entrance fee station and turn left at a pullout for the Natural Arches/Charlie's Spring trailhead. If you're driving from the eastern entrance, drive 0.7 mile west from the fee station and turn right into the parking area. Do not block access to the service road.

Trail Description

Fire Canyon isn't quite in the realm of technical canyoneering but is an excellent adventure. This is an advanced hike with some tricky downclimbs and possible navigation challenges to bypass some potentially wet potholes. There are some splendid, scenic side canyons that are worth spending some extra time to explore. This hike also requires the use of a car shuttle.

From the Mouse's Tank parking lot, hike east down a sidewalk which quickly ends in a sandy wash. An easy, short sandy hike down-canyon takes you to Mouse's Tank. Keep your eyes open as there are numerous petroglyphs along the trail. Bypass Mouse's Tank on the left via a series of easy slabs and return back into the wash.

Continuing down wash, the canyon temporarily narrows and a mandatory eight foot, class 4, downclimb will be required off a boulder. Once the canyon widens, another dryfall is encountered which is easily bypassed on the left.

Surrounded by fantastic red rock peaks, the hike becomes a sandy trek. After 1.9 miles, a short narrow section of canyon marks the beginning of the next set of obstacles. A slim slot-like dryfall is met which is bypassed via an easy downclimb on the left. Shortly thereafter, the canyon walls rise and slots up.

A tricky downclimb is required into a pothole. If this pothole is full of water, muddy or you don't like the downclimb take the described bypass. Once in the pothole, a tough elevator style downclimb is required to the bottom of the slot. If there has been any precipitation recently, the bottom of this climb will be wet and muddy. Moreover, if you're not accustomed to canyoneering downclimbing, these will be difficult.

If you want to bypass this section, before the downclimb into the pothole, backtrack up-canyon for 100 feet and look (south) for an easy exit on the left (looking up-canyon). Climb up some slickrock to a sandy garden and then hike south-southeast to intercept a southwest-northeast side joint. Descend northeast into this side joint where a downclimb leads back to the main wash.

Amazing narrows follow the pothole downclimb; it's too bad they don't last longer! The canyon widens and after another 1.4 miles, you'll intersect the end of the Natural Arches trail. Keep your eyes open for interesting rock features and arches. The last 0.8 mile to the car is painfully sandy.

Before crossing under the Valley of Fire Highway, exit Fire Wash via a trail on the right that parallels the paved road which will take you to the car shuttle parking.

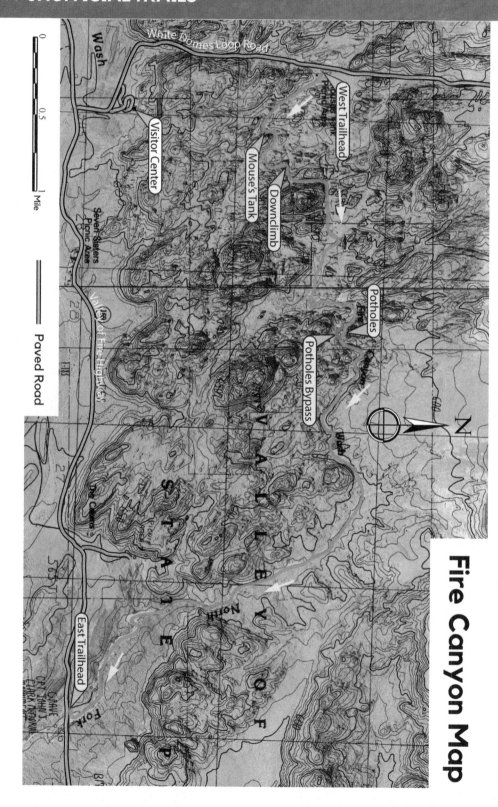

Fire Canyon Map

"The Orphan"

Chapter 3

Introduction to Peaks

Most of these peaks are not suitable for casual hikers. Venturing prepared with a solid base of experience will make these peaks rewarding and enjoyable adventures. The highest quality panoramic vistas in the park await your arrival on the summit. These peaks require self reliance, excellent judgment, knowledge, scrambling and off-route navigational experience.

Disclaimer: It should be noted that all peak names and other names in quotations are unoffical, informal names. In case of emergency, it is best to provide the park with GPS coordinates as the park may not be aware of or acknowledge these locations.

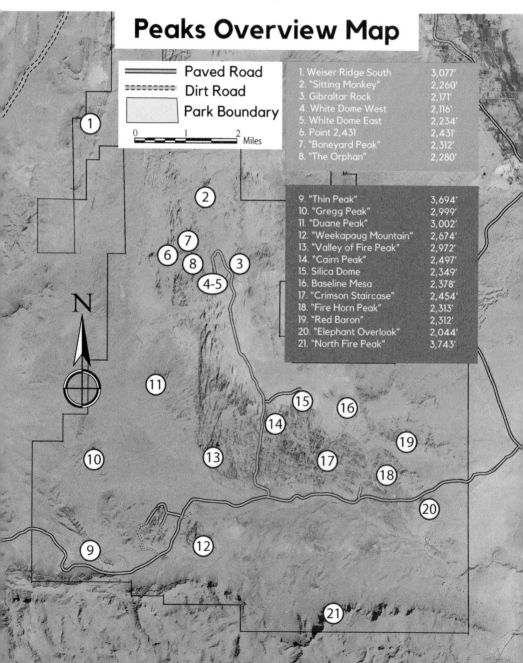

Peaks Overview Map

———	Paved Road
---------	Dirt Road
☐	Park Boundary

0   1   2 Miles

#	Name	Elevation
1.	Weiser Ridge South	3,077'
2.	"Sitting Monkey"	2,260'
3.	Gibraltar Rock	2,171'
4.	White Dome West	2,116'
5.	White Dome East	2,234'
6.	Point 2,431	2,431'
7.	"Boneyard Peak"	2,312'
8.	"The Orphan"	2,280'
9.	"Thin Peak"	3,694'
10.	"Gregg Peak"	2,999'
11.	"Duane Peak"	3,002'
12.	"Weekapaug Mountain"	2,674'
13.	"Valley of Fire Peak"	2,972'
14.	"Cairn Peak"	2,497'
15.	Silica Dome	2,349'
16.	Baseline Mesa	2,378'
17.	"Crimson Staircase"	2,454'
18.	"Fire Horn Peak"	2,313'
19.	"Red Baron"	2,312'
20.	"Elephant Overlook"	2,044'
21.	"North Fire Peak"	3,743'

N

WEISER RIDGE SOUTH   3,077′

Weiser Ridge has several summits stretching to the north creating the western edge of "the valley." The southern point of Weiser Ridge is barely within park boundaries and is best accessed from the west off the Ute exit on I-15. Gaining the summit gives one a different perspective on the park and is probably best reserved for list chasing peak baggers.

WEST SLOPES, CLASS 2

Distance: ~3.2 Miles	Time Required: 1-2 Hours
Elevation Gain: ~700 Feet	Rating: ★ ★ ☆ ☆ ☆

Driving Directions

Take exit 80 from I-15. Starting at the cattle guard on the southeast side of the highway, drive 6.2 miles on a well maintained gravel road. You will know you are on the correct road if you see a sign marked "Weiser Quarry 7 Miles."

Turn right onto a high clearance road and drive 0.4 mile to a wash. This is the trailhead. If you drive past a small red sandstone tower on the right or reach a second wash, you have driven too far. 2WD vehicles should park at a gravel pullout before the high clearance road.

Route

From the parking area, follow the wash southeast then east towards the peak. As you hike farther up the wash, the wash transitions into an ATV road. Continue to follow the ATV road east until it intersects a north-south ATV road. Cross this road and start cross-country hiking towards the base of the west slopes of Weiser Ridge. Hike or scramble up a series of gullies to the summit.

Just before reaching the summit, there is a small cliff band which guards easy access to the top. Hike/traverse south along the base of the cliff band where a weakness can be found leading to the summit. Enjoy the views of Weiser Quarry and the park of this seldom visited perch.

Sunrise on the summit of Weiser Ridge

Weiser Ridge South Map

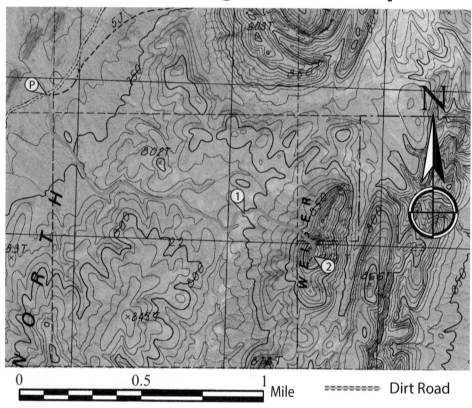

0   0.5   1 Mile   ▱▱▱▱▱▱▱ Dirt Road

Key Waypoints	Longitude	Latitude
Ⓟ▷ Parking/Trailhead	N36.5363	W114.6014
①▷ ATV Road Junction	N36.5285	W114.5878
②▷ Summit	N36.5270	W114.5820

"SITTING MONKEY"   2,260'

Anchoring the north end of the red rock peaks, Sitting Monkey offers two high quality scrambling routes. Contrasting colors of white domes, orange and red sandstone create a fantastic summit vista. Spend an extra 15 minutes on the approach or return to visit Duck Rock.

EAST SLOPES, CLASS 3

Distance: ~2.9 Miles   Time Required: 2-3 Hours
Elevation Gain: ~700 Feet   Rating: ★ ★ ★ ☆ ☆

Driving Directions

From the beginning of the White Domes Loop road, drive 5.2 miles north to a pullout for a closed road on the right. This is the most northern curve, before the road turns back south for the White Domes, on the White Domes Loop road.

Route

From the parking area, start hiking north on a closed road. When you have reached the end of the well established road descend into and cross Magnesite Wash. Search for and follow an ATV road heading north out of the wash. Keep an eye out for another ATV road to your left after you have exited the wash. Take this ATV road left as it almost makes a u-turn and heads southwest up a hill. The road then turns west which will take you to the south side of the peak.

Once on the south side of the peak, leave the ATV road and scramble north up a gully splitting the two summits to the saddle. From the saddle, follow a ledge (left) southwest to the base of a headwall. Climb straight up the headwall (class 3-4) to a bench which is then followed by more class 3 scrambling to the summit.

SOUTH RIDGE VARIATION, CLASS 4

Distance: ~2.9 Miles
Elevation Gain: ~700 Feet
Time Required: 2-3 Hours
Rating: ★ ★ ★ ★ ☆

For a more sustained scrambling adventure, this is a good route. Follow the East Slope route to the base of the gully splitting the two summits. Climb halfway up the gully and search for a ledge leading to the south ridge. Traverse across the semi-exposed ledge to the ridge and then follow the path of least resistance up a slab to the ridge proper (class 4). The ridge will then guide you to the summit (class 3). Descend the East Slopes.

"Sitting Monkey" 2,260'
East Slopes, Class 3
South Ridge, Class 4

Summit
East Slopes
South Ridge

"Sitting Monkey" Map

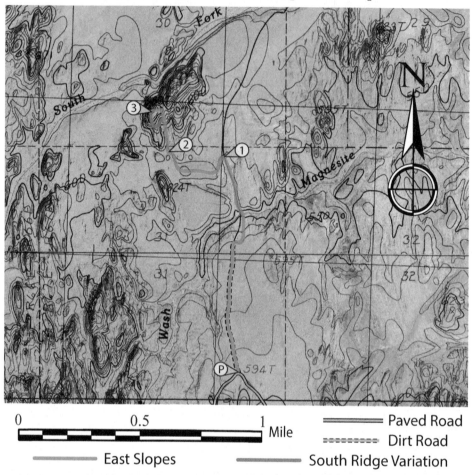

		0	0.5	1 Mile

━━━━━ Paved Road	
⚎⚎⚎⚎⚎ Dirt Road	
───── East Slopes	───── South Ridge Variation

Key Waypoints	Longitude	Latitude
Ⓟ Trailhead/Parking	N36.4932	W114.5318
① ATV Road Junction	N36.5055	W114.5330
② Base of Gully	N36.5060	W114.5372
③ Summit	N36.5081	W114.5384

GIBRALTAR ROCK   2,171'

Gibraltar Rock is a striking red rock prow that lines the eastern horizon at the Fire Wave trailhead. This highly enjoyable scramble makes for a great outing by itself but combines well if you're interested in visiting the Fire Wave.

Photo by Holly Gilhart-Wolfe

EAST SLOPES, CLASS 4

Distance: ~1.6 Miles   **Time Required: 1-2 Hours**
Elevation Gain: ~450 Feet   **Rating: ★ ★ ★ ★ ☆**

Driving Directions

From the beginning of the White Domes Loop road, drive 4.8 miles north to the well marked Fire Wave trailhead on the left.

Route

Map on page 54

Various routes gain the summit of Gibraltar Rock. The route described is low impact and stays out of view from other park visitors. From the Fire Wave parking lot, begin hiking down the sandy Fire Wave trail. Once on the south side of Gibraltar Rock, there will be a faint trail junction after 0.4 mile. The Fire Wave trail continues right, go left up this unmarked trail as it climbs a small hill on the east side of Gibraltar Rock.

At the top of the hill, leave the trail heading west, across some slickrock to a gully that provides access through a cliff band on Gibraltar's east face. Your objective is to enter a large narrow canyon that splits the entire rock formation. Route finding into this canyon can be tricky. Climb up the gully to the top and then make a descending u-turn which will allow you to enter the large narrow canyon.

Descend halfway down the narrow canyon looking for the first climbable, right facing slickrock dihedral/ramp on the left (west). Climb up the slabby ramp (class 4) which provides access to the top of the canyon's walls. From the top of the ramp, scramble west through a series of slickrock fins and gullies to the top (class 3). A lofty perch that overlooks the Fire Wave awaits your arrival.

WEST WHITE DOME

2,116'

Sustained, exposed scrambling makes this one of the highest quality quick scrambles in the park. Too bad it's not longer. While you're at it, climb East White Dome too.

NORTH RIDGE, CLASS 3

Distance: ~0.3 Mile

Elevation Gain: ~100 Feet

Time Required: 15-30 Minutes

Rating: ★ ★ ★ ★ ☆

Driving Directions

From the beginning of the White Domes Loop road, drive 5.7 miles north to the well marked White Domes Loop trailhead. This is the end of the road.

Route

Map on page 54

Almost the entire route can be viewed from the White Domes Loop parking area. From the parking area, locate a dominant gully up the north side of the dome. Scramble up a slick-rock ramp on the right (west) side of the gully to enter the gully with ease. Once in the gully, scramble upwards until the gully terminates. Exit the gully (right) onto a narrow exposed ledge and follow the ledge south until you're able to scamper onto the ridge proper.

Now for the best part, scramble along the narrow summit ridge to the tippy-top. It's an abrupt drop-off on all sides.

Summit of East White Dome

EAST WHITE DOME   2,234'

Although not as exciting as its western counterpart, East White Dome is an exciting quick scramble and should not be missed. To maximize your scramble, it is best combined with West White Dome.

NORTH RIDGE, CLASS 4

Distance: ~0.4 Mile	Time Required: 20-40 Minutes
Elevation Gain: ~250 Feet	Rating: ★ ★ ★ ☆ ☆

Driving Directions

From the beginning of the White Domes Loop road, drive 5.7 miles north to the well marked White Domes Loop trailhead. This is the end of the road.

Route

Map on page 54

From the parking area, scramble up an easy slickrock ramp to the base of the north ridge where a cliff bars easy access to the upper ramparts of the dome. Locate a slot-like chimney on the west side of the cliff which can be easily identified by a small bush at its base. Traverse south into the chimney and carefully stem up the chimney, class 4. Once out of the chimney, some occasional class 3 scrambling along the ridge crest will guide you to the summit. A sea of vibrant orange, red and white sandstone formations await your summit arrival.

WHITE DOMES COMBO, CLASS 4

Distance: ~0.7 Mile	Time Required: 30 Minutes-1 Hour
Elevation Gain: ~350 Feet	Rating: ★ ★ ★ ★ ★

Climb the north ridge route on West White Dome and then traverse across the White Domes Loop parking lot and climb the north ridge on East White Dome.

White Domes & Gibraltar Rock Map

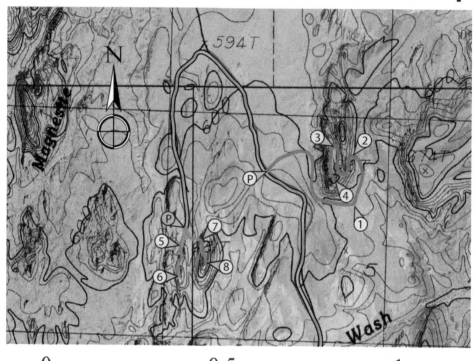

Key Waypoints		Longitude	Latitude
(P)	Parking - Gibraltar Rock	N36.4883	W114.5286
(1)	Trail Junction	N36.4870	W114.5246
(2)	Base of Gully, Gibraltar Rock	N36.4887	W114.5244
(3)	Start of Class 4 Slab	N36.4890	W114.5251
(4)	Summit of Gibraltar Rock	N36.4878	W114.5255
(P)	Parking - White Domes	N36.4858	W114.5329
(5)	Base of N Ridge, W White Dome	N36.4856	W114.5331
(6)	Summit of W White Dome	N36.4841	W114.5333
(7)	Base of Chimney, E White Dome	N36.4858	W114.5320
(8)	Summit of E White Dome	N36.4846	W114.5318

POINT 2,431

2,431'

Somewhat secluded, this stoic peak is the furthest western red sandstone peak in the park. Point 2,431 is usually combined with The Orphan and Boneyard Peak for a fantastic scramble linkup. You'll also have the opportunity to explore the headwaters of Magnesite Wash on the approach.

SOUTH SLOPES, CLASS 3

Distance: ~3.0 Miles
Elevation Gain: ~500 Feet

Time Required: 1.5-2 Hours
Rating: ★ ★ ★ ☆ ☆

Driving Directions

From the beginning of the White Domes Loop road, drive 5.7 miles north to the well marked White Domes Loop trailhead. This is the end of the road.

Route

Map on page 59

Start by hiking the White Domes Loop trail counterclockwise. Once on the northwest side of a prominent white dome, 0.25 mile from the trailhead, depart the trail hiking west. Once you intercept Magnesite Wash, continue hiking west staying in the wash. A few wet pools may be encountered which can easily be bypassed. Determining when to leave Magnesite Wash for Point 2,431 can be tricky and it's best to leave it when you're directly south of the peak when it becomes less featured.

After you leave Magnesite Wash, hike north to the base of 2,431's south gully. Take the furthest right (east) gully on the west side of the summit block. Scramble up and over boulders to the top of the gully (class 2). Once at the top of the gully, traverse on a small ledge to the north side of the peak and squeeze up an improbable chimney (class 3) which will lead you to the summit.

Be cautious of loose boulders at the top of the chimney. The views of the park to the south are supreme.

Point 2,431 from the south

Summit view from Point 2.431

"BONEYARD PEAK" 2,312'

Boneyard Peak offers solitude and some interesting scrambling to its summit. There is also the option for a quick detour into a very short, scenic, non-technical slot canyon. Due to Boneyard Peak's proximity to The Orphan, they are best completed as a combo climb.

EAST SLOPES, CLASS 4

Distance: ~3.4 Miles
Elevation Gain: ~600 Feet

Time Required: 1.5-2 Hours
Rating: ★ ★ ★ ☆ ☆

Driving Directions

From the beginning of the White Domes Loop road, drive 5.7 miles north to the well marked White Domes Loop trailhead. This is the end of the road.

Route
Map on page 59

Start by hiking the White Domes Loop trail counterclockwise. Once on the northwest side of a prominent white dome, 0.25 mile from the trailhead, depart the trail hiking west. Cross a very minor wash and continue cross-country hiking west towards the south side of The Orphan. Once you intersect Magnesite Wash, hike between two smaller red rock ridges to the southwest side of The Orphan. Don't take the first tributary north on the west side of The Orphan but instead take the second. Hike north up the second tributary wash as you go up and over a small saddle to the southern edge of Boneyard.

A large gully splits Boneyard's southern flanks. Scramble up this gully, bypassing several large boulders, to an amphitheater at the top. The key to reaching the summit of Boneyard lies in this amphitheater.

Climb up a large crack in the southwestern corner of the amphitheater to a slickrock bench located above the amphitheater (class 4) and then traverse north along the slickrock bench towards the summit. Some final scrambling though a rock fin and summit ramp lead to the top (class 3).

If you want to visit an interesting short slot canyon, from the amphitheater, continue north in the gully and search for the entrance to the slot canyon on the right (east). You can descend the narrow canyon, reaching a wash which flows back into Magnesite Wash. Carefully route find your way back to the paved road or White Domes Loop trail which will take you back to the trailhead.

"THE ORPHAN" 2,280'

Nestled between red rock gargoyles, The Orphan guards its unlikely summit passage for those seeking a route finding adventure. The lofty summit offers phenomenal views of the White Domes.

NORTH RIDGE, CLASS 3

Distance: ~3.2 Miles
Elevation Gain: ~500 Feet

Time Required: 1.5-2 Hours
Rating: ★ ★ ★ ★ ☆

Driving Directions

From the beginning of the White Domes Loop road, drive 5.7 miles north to the well marked White Domes Loop trailhead. This is the end of the road.

Route

Start by hiking the White Domes Loop trail counterclockwise. Once on the northwest side of a prominent white dome, 0.25 mile from the trailhead, depart the trail hiking west. Cross a very minor wash and continue cross-country hiking west towards the south side of the peak. Once you arrive at Magnesite Wash, hike between two smaller red rock ridges to the southwest side of the peak. Don't take the first tributary north on the west side of the peak but instead take the second. Hike north up the second tributary wash as you go up and over a small saddle. Work around to the northwest side of the peak to an obvious shallow gully.

Scramble up the shallow gully as it intersects another deeper gully. Continue upward in the second deeper gully until it terminates; then follow a slickrock ramp up and right to the base of The Orphan's north ridge. A short section of class 3 face climbing intercepts the north ridge proper. Either climb the ridge directly (class 3-4) or chimney up a shallow slot (class 3).

Once you reach the final summit block, traverse on a somewhat exposed ledge along the west side. After you pass a small cove, then climb the face to the summit (class 3). The southern summit is higher.

THE FULL MONTY, CLASS 4

Distance: ~6.0 Miles
Elevation Gain: ~2,100 Feet

Time Required: 3.5-6 Hours
Rating: ★ ★ ★ ★ ★

This is the finest scrambling linkup in the park and the best way to combine The White Domes, Point 2,431, The Orphan, and Boneyard Peak. From the trailhead, complete the White Domes duo. Then climb the south slopes on Point 2,431, return back down Magnesite Wash, take the tributary wash described for the The Orphan and climb Boneyard's south slopes and then finish on The Orphan's north ridge.

"The Orphan," "Boneyard Peak," Point 2,431 Map

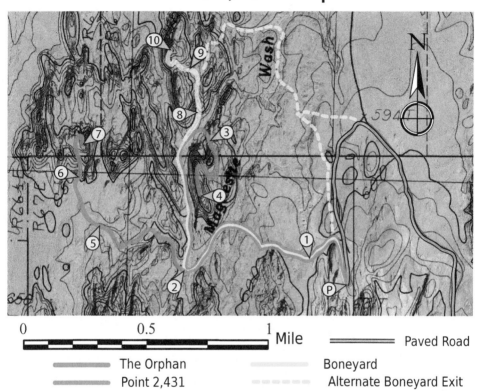

0	0.5	1 Mile

The Orphan
Point 2,431

Boneyard
Alternate Boneyard Exit

Paved Road

Key Waypoints	Longitude	Latitude
P ▷ Parking - White Domes	N36.4861	W114.5329
1 ▷ Leave White Domes Loop Trail	N36.4874	W114.5347
2 ▷ Leave Magnesite Wash, Orphan/Boneyard	N36.4868	W114.5415
3 ▷ Base of North Gully, The Orphan	N36.4930	W114.5404
4 ▷ Summit of The Orphan	N36.4902	W114.5409
5 ▷ Leave Magnesite Wash, Pt 2,431	N36.4885	W114.5469
6 ▷ Base of South Gully, Point 2,431	N36.4907	W114.5477
7 ▷ Summit of Point 2,431	N36.4919	W114.5474
8 ▷ Base of South Gully, Boneyard	N36.4933	W114.5410
9 ▷ Amphitheater, Boneyard	N36.4950	W114.5414
10 ▷ Summit of Boneyard	N36.4962	W114.5426

En route to The Orphan

"Fire Horn Peak"

Chapter 4

"THIN PEAK"

3,694'

One of the highest peaks in the park—anchoring the southwest corner—the summit of Thin Peak offers outstanding views of the expansive red sandstone peaks to the east. To the north, the hidden Pinnacles show their majestic beauty. As you enter the park from the west, Thin Peak is one of the first peaks you'll see.

SOUTHWEST SLOPES, CLASS 2

Distance: ~1.0 Mile
Elevation Gain: ~700 Feet

Time Required: 30 Minutes - 1 Hour
Rating: ★ ★ ★ ☆ ☆

Driving Directions

This trailhead is located outside of the western fee station. From the western fee station drive west 1.5 miles up a large "S" turn to a gravel pullout on the south side of the road at the top of a hill. This is the trailhead.

Route

Although not an exciting scramble, this peak is short and offers fantastic views. Starting from the parking area, cross-country hike to the base of the southwest slopes of Thin and choose a line up one of the various ridges. Intersect the northwest ridge and hike up a narrow, semi-exposed ridge to the top. The views of the Pinnacles are great.

The Pinnacles and Gregg Peak viewed from the summit of Thin Peak.

"Thin Peak" Map

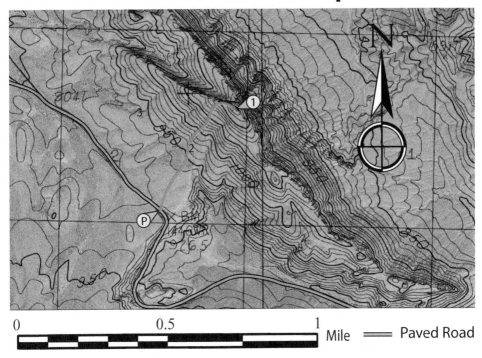

| 0 | 0.5 | 1 | Mile | ━━ Paved Road |

Key Waypoints	Latitude	Longitude
(P)▷ Parking/Trailhead	N36.4111	W114.5859
(1)▷ Summit	N36.4159	W114.5814

"GREGG PEAK"   2,999'

This peak should be reserved for the hardened peak bagging connoisseurs. If you do decide to climb this peak, it is best to combine this peak with the Pinnacles Loop trail. Despite the poor quality rock and unexciting climbing, the views of the Pinnacles from the top almost make this peak a worthy side trip.

EAST SLOPES, CLASS 2

Distance: ~4.2 Miles   Time Required: 2-3 Hours
Elevation Gain: ~800 Feet   Rating: ★ ☆ ☆ ☆ ☆

Driving Directions

Drive 1.8 miles east on the Valley of Fire highway from the west entrance fee station and turn left on a paved road for Atlatl Rock and The Scenic Loop. If you're driving from the eastern entrance, drive 5.2 miles west from the fee station and turn right onto the road. Continue 0.5 mile on the Scenic Loop and make a left to the Atlatl Rock picnic area parking.

Route

From the Atlatl Rock parking area, cross the Scenic Loop road and look for a poorly marked trailhead for the Pinnacles Loop Trail. If your sole objective is Gregg, hike the Pinnacles Loop counterclockwise until you're directly east of the peak. Leave the Pinnacles Loop trail and cross-country hike to Gregg's east slopes. Choose a line up the fractured slopes that will intercept Gregg's south ridge. Be cautious of loose rock as you hike up to the top.

Once intersecting the south ridge, the rock quality becomes better. The views of the Pinnacles from the summit are inspiring.

If you're combining this peak with the Pinnacles Loop, it's best to add this peak after visiting the Pinnacles and to hike the Pinnacles Loop clockwise. Do not be tempted to climb the west slopes of Gregg from the Pinnacles; it has some of the worst rock quality I have found in the park.

"Gregg Peak" Map

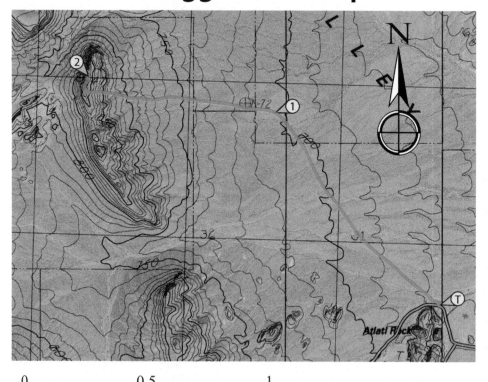

| 0 | 0.5 | 1 Mile | ══════ Paved Road |

Key Waypoints		Latitude	Longitude
T	Trailhead	N36.4245	W114.5511
1	Leave Pinnacles Loop	N36.4348	W114.5620
2	Summit	N36.4368	W114.5766

"DUANE PEAK"

3,002'

Somewhat isolated, this peak should be tackled after climbing all other peaks in the park. The views of Valley of Fire Peak and White Domes make this excursion somewhat of a worthy expedition.

SOUTHEAST SLOPES, CLASS 2

Distance: ~5.6 Miles	Time Required: 2.5-4 Hours
Elevation Gain: ~1,200 Feet	Rating: ★ ☆ ☆ ☆ ☆

Driving Directions

Drive 2.2 miles east on the Valley of Fire highway from the western entrance fee station and turn left at a pullout for the Prospect Trail trailhead. If you're driving from the eastern entrance, drive 4.8 miles west from the fee station and turn right into the parking area.

Route

Starting from the southern Prospect Trail trailhead, follow the well-maintained gravel service road, part of the Prospect Trail, for 0.4 mile. When the service road turns east, continue to follow the Prospect Trail north.

The trail passes through an area of featured red rocks as it crests a small hill. As the trail starts to descend on the other side of the hill, cross a small wash and look for an abandoned 4x4 road on the left (west) side of the trail. The road junction is 1.8 miles from the trailhead. Take the old 4x4 road west as it climbs up a small hill. Continue to follow the road as it turns north and crosses a few small drainages. When the road ends, climb directly west to Duane's southeast ridge. If you climb directly toward Duane's summit, not recommended, from the end of the road, you will cross several annoying drainages.

Once gaining Duane's southeast ridge, hike northwest up the ridge to the summit where the hiking becomes more enjoyable. At least the views to the northeast are decent.

"Duane Peak" Map

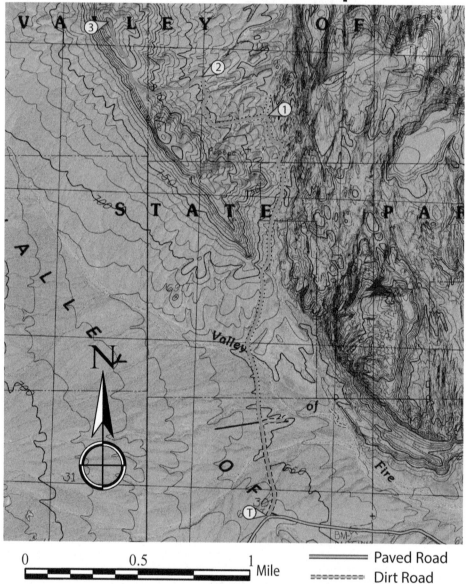

	0	0.5	1 Mile		Paved Road
					Dirt Road

Key Waypoints		Latitude	Longitude
T	Trailhead	N36.4263	W114.5404
1	Old 4x4 Road Junction	N36.4507	W114.5410
2	End of Road	N36.4530	W114.5460
3	Summit	N36.4565	W114.5535

"WEEKAPAUG MOUNTAIN" 2,674'

Weekapaug is the prominently striking red peak on the south side of the Valley of Fire highway near the western entrance. At first glance there doesn't seem to be an easy way to the top, but this peak offers a great introduction to class 3. It is also a great introduction to harder route finding and navigation without the consequences of getting too lost.

"Weekapaug Mountain"

NORTHEAST SLOPES, CLASS 2

Distance: ~1.4 Miles	Time Required: 1-2 Hours
Elevation Gain: ~700 Feet	Rating: ★ ★ ★ ☆ ☆

Driving Directions

Drive 1.8 miles east on the Valley of Fire highway from the west entrance fee station and turn right on the Petrified Logs Loop road (dirt). If you're driving from the eastern entrance, drive 5.2 miles west from the fee station and turn left onto the Petrified Logs Loop road (dirt). Continue an additional 0.2 mile to the parking area for the Petrified Logs.

Route

From the West Petrified Log parking area, hike in the open desert southeast towards the base of the north ridge of Weekapaug. Circumnavigate clockwise around the base of the peak until reaching the first reasonable gully that can be ascended, located on the northeast side of the peak. Climb this gully to a long north-south cliff band which guards access to the summit area. Locate a thin keyhole notch in this cliff band and climb through the notch. Climbing at this point should not exceed class 2.

Once through the notch, make a quick U-turn, back north, leading to an upper desert garden and the summit massive. Several red sandstone fins make it hard to locate the true summit. Scramble south up the central red fin where a small notch, just before the summit, bars access to the top. Descend into the notch and then enjoy a short class 3 ramp to the summit.

"Weekapaug Mountain" Map

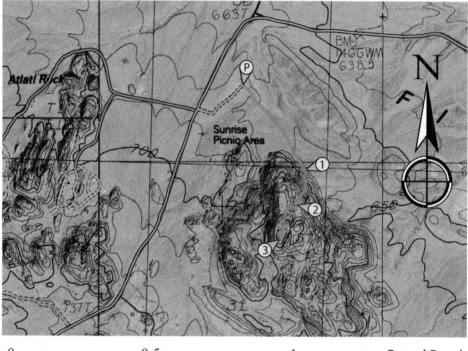

	0	0.5	1 Mile

	Paved Road
	Dirt Road

Key Waypoints		Latitude	Longitude
P	Trailhead/Parking	N36.4226	W114.5413
1	Base of gully	N36.4187	W114.5376
2	"Keyhole"	N36.4166	W114.5378
3	Summit	N36.4149	W114.5390

"VALLEY OF FIRE PEAK"   2,972'

This peak has the most challenging route finding of any peak in the park. The labyrinth of red sandstone fins guarding the summit makes travel complicated and navigation difficult. Expect arduous route finding and allow extra time. The rewards for reaching the summit are astonishing 360 degree views of the park. Welcome to the maze.

SOUTH RIDGE, CLASS 4

Distance: ~4.4 Miles	Time Required: 3-5 Hours
Elevation Gain: ~1,200 Feet	Rating: ★ ★ ★ ★ ★

Driving Directions

From the beginning of the White Domes Loop road, drive 1.0 mile north. Park at a single car pullout on the left. If you reach Mouse's Tank trailhead, you've gone too far; backtrack 0.2 mile. If the parking spot is occupied, park at Mouse's Tank trailhead.

Route

From the parking area, hike west up a small canyon where some minor boulder-hopping is required. Before reaching the end of the canyon, look for a side canyon/ramp on the left (south). Make a 120 degree turn and follow the ramp southeast to the top of a flat plateau that is riddled with red rock fins. This is where route finding can become tricky. Navigate south/southeast until intercepting a prominent wash.

Once you reach the wash, hike south up the wash where some pools and short dryfalls will be encountered. These can easily be by-passed with trivial scrambling on either side. Continue following the wash as it makes a turn to the west; near the end, staying in the most prominent drainage becomes challenging. You are aiming for a larger open basin directly east of the large summit massive.

After navigating the open basin, hike south and then west to reach the base of Valley of Fire Peak's south ridge. There are two options for gaining the ridge. Either follow an angling left ramp with vegetation and some boulders (class 2) or a more aesthetic series of clean slabs (5.2) that lead to a small notch in the ridge.

Once on Valley of Fire Peak's south ridge, traverse on the west side of the ridge to a deep in-cut gully. Climb up the gully (class 3) which can be sandy. At the top, go right for

The deep in-cut gully on Valley of Fire's south ridge

100 feet and climb a short exposed class 4 step to regain the south ridge proper.

Romp north along the top of the south ridge until reaching a deep notch in the ridge. Descend into the notch, look for a rock pile step and climb up the opposite wall. The climb up the opposite wall is at an improbable location but will guide you to a narrow ledge that escapes the notch to the left (class 4).

Continue to follow the south ridge once you're out of the notch where some short slabby class 3 sections will be encountered before reaching the summit. Don't forget to pack a lunch to enjoy at one of the several picnic tables located on the summit plateau.

NORTH RIDGE, CLASS 3

Distance: ~5.6 Miles
Elevation Gain: ~1,400 Feet

Time Required: 3-5 Hours
Rating: ★ ★ ★ ★ ☆

Valley of Fire Peak's north ridge

Driving Directions

Drive 2.2 miles east on the Valley of Fire highway from the west entrance fee station and turn left at a pullout for the Prospect Trail trailhead. If you're driving from the eastern entrance, drive 4.8 miles west from the fee station and turn right into the parking area.

Route

Starting from the southern Prospect Trail trailhead, follow the well maintained gravel service road, part of the Prospect Trail, for 0.4 mile. When the service road turns east, continue to follow the Prospect Trail north.

After 1.3 miles, as the Prospect Trail enters an area of featured red rock, look for a wash that closely parallels the trail. Leave the Prospect Trail and hike up the wash as it turns around and heads southeast up a large gully towards Valley of Fire Peak. This gully is the only weakness through the large rock band and is not easily identified from the southern side of the Prospect Trail. If you continue up the Prospect Trail too far, you will be able to identify the gully easier but expect some boulder hoping and route finding back into the gully.

Climb up the gully, some minor class 3 through some boulders, where the hard route finding begins. Your objective is to find a somewhat narrow canyon directly north of the summit massive. First, you must cross a few sandstone fins and high gardens where there is no obvious way. A GPS is extremely helpful in this very complex terrain.

A wide, large garden is a clue that you are close to the mouth of the narrow canyon and once you have identified the narrow canyon, make an arduous bushwhack south up the canyon towards the base of Valley of Fire Peak's north ridge.

Pick your line out of the canyon carefully as not all of the slickrock ridges provide direct access to Valley of Fire Peak's north ridge. After you have found a path through the slickrock fins, a steep exposed class 3 step is required to reach the upper flanks of the ridge.

Once on the upper flanks, easy, steep slickrock hiking leads to the summit. The views make the bushwhack worthwhile.

If you're interested in a quick side trip to an amazing non-technical slot canyon, continue hiking up the narrow canyon before the slickrock ridge to the start of the slot canyon on the left. It might take a little effort to find. Make sure to return the same way you came as descending the other side of the canyon is a horrific bushwhack.

"Valley of Fire Peak" Map

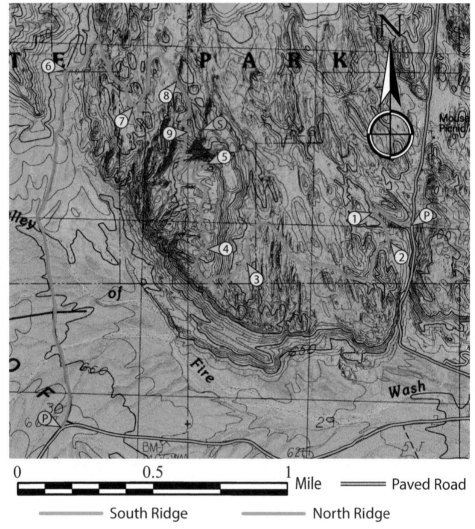

0   0.5   1 Mile   ══ Paved Road

══ South Ridge   ══ North Ridge

Valley of Fire Peak from the north

Key Waypoints	Latitude	Longitude
P Parking/Trailhead - S Ridge	N36.4362	W114.5177
1 Base of Ramp in First Canyon	N36.4374	W114.5202
2 Start of Wash After Ramp	N36.4357	W114.5193
3 Open Basin East of Summit	N36.4344	W114.5288
4 Class 4 Step	N36.4353	W114.5311
5 Summit	N36.4393	W114.5311
P Parking/Trailhead - N Ridge	N36.4263	W114.5404
6 Leave Prospect Trail	N36.4446	W114.5404
7 Top of Gully	N36.4425	W114.5357
8 Mouth of Narrow Canyon	N36.4438	W114.5332
9 Start of Slickrock	N36.4419	W114.5325
S Slot Canyon Side Trip	N36.4410	W114.5316

Side slot

"CAIRN PEAK"

2,497'

Easily combined with the Rainbow Vista trail, this peak is a quick excursion. Due to Cairn's central location, the summit provides excellent panoramas of Silica Dome, Valley of Fire Peak and Fire Canyon. This is also one of the easiest peak scrambles in the book.

NORTH RIDGE, CLASS 3

Distance: ~0.9 Mile	Time Required: 30-45 Minutes
Elevation Gain: ~400 Feet	Rating: ★ ★ ★ ☆ ☆

Driving Directions

From the beginning of the White Domes Loop road, drive 1.9 miles north to the well marked Rainbow Vista trailhead.

Route

Begin east down the Rainbow Vista trail for 200 yards to an open meadow north of the peak. Leave the trail and start hiking south in a small wash until you intersect Cairn Peak's north ridge. With careful route finding, only a few minor sections of class 3 scrambling on the ridge will be required to reach the summit. Harder scrambling options exist. This route is a great introduction to class 3 since the sections of class 3 are short and not exposed.

"Cairn Peak" Map

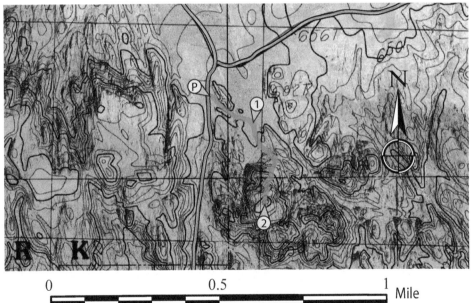

0	0.5	1	Mile

═══ Paved Road

Key Waypoints	Latitude	Longitude
P ▷ Trailhead/Parking	N36.4509	W114.5154
1 ▷ Leave the Trail	N36.4500	W 114.5134
2 ▷ Summit	N36.4467	W114.5126

SILICA DOME

2,349'

Making for a short hike, this peak offers fantastic views of the surrounding red rock landscapes in minimal time. Despite being un-ranked, there is a sense of accomplishment as the south face of Silica Dome promptly drops off further than you have climbed.

NORTH RIDGE, CLASS 2

Distance: ~1.0 Mile	Time Required: 30-45 Minutes
Elevation Gain: ~250 Feet	Rating: ★ ★ ★ ☆ ☆

Driving Directions

From the beginning of the White Domes Loop road, drive 2.0 miles north. Turn right onto the Fire Canyon/Silica Dome Road and drive 0.8 mile to the Fire Canyon/Silica Dome overlook parking.

Route

From the Silica Dome parking area, follow an old road for 0.2 mile until you're directly north of the summit. Take a trail that splits south from the road that heads to the north ridge of the peak. Interesting white rock features guide you to the summit. There are fantastic views of Fire Canyon on this lofty vista.

Photo by Holly Gilhart Wolfe

BASELINE MESA 2,378'

Despite the unattractive hike, the views from the summit looking south are appealing. This peak is only recommended for desperate peak baggers.

NORTHWEST SLOPES, CLASS 2

Distance: ~3.8 Miles	Time Required: 2-3 Hours
Elevation Gain: ~800 Feet	Rating: ★ ★ ☆ ☆ ☆

Driving Directions

From the beginning of the White Domes Loop road, drive 2.0 miles north. Turn right onto the Fire Canyon/Silica Dome Road and drive 0.8 mile to the Fire Canyon/Silica Dome overlook parking.

Route

From the Silica Dome parking area, hike east following an old road for 1.1 miles as it descends into an unappealing, desolate valley. Depart the road once you're on the northwest side of the mesa before the road starts heading north. There is a very faint road leading south to a wash. Follow the faint road, cross the wash and navigate through a red rock layer to gain the top of the mesa. Good route finding will keep the route at class 2. Once you penetrate through the limestone rim at the top of the mesa, a gentle hike southeast leads to the summit.

Baseline Mesa & Silica Dome Map

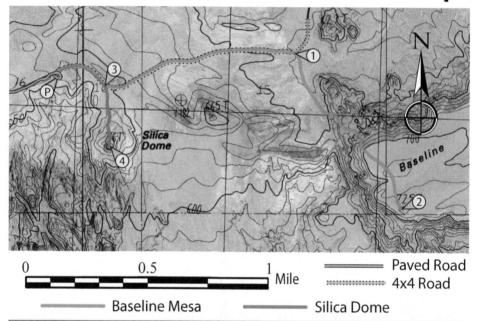

0	0.5	1 Mile	

══════ Paved Road
∙∙∙∙∙∙∙∙∙∙∙ 4x4 Road

══════ Baseline Mesa   ══════ Silica Dome

Key Waypoints		Latitude	Longitude
P	Trailhead/Parking	N36.4556	W114.5023
1	Leave the Road, Baseline Mesa	N36.4571	W114.4850
2	Summit of Baseline Mesa	N36.4479	W114.4772
3	Leave the Road, Silica Dome	N36.4552	W114.4995
4	Summit of Silica Dome	N36.4517	W114.4989

Scrambling on Crimson Staircase

"CRIMSON STAIRCASE" 2,454'

Nestled deep in a majestic sea of red rock peaks, Crimson Staircase offers a refreshing canyon approach hike with mind-blowing landscapes. An improbable path surprisingly leads to the summit. For those seeking a shorter alternative, Crimson Staircase can also be accessed via the Valley of Fire highway.

SOUTHWEST SLOPES VIA FIRE CANYON, CLASS 4

Distance: ~5.1 Miles
Elevation Gain: ~1,100 Feet

Time Required: 3-4 Hours
Rating: ★ ★ ★ ★ ☆

Driving Directions

From the beginning of the White Domes Loop road, drive 1.2 miles north and make a right turn to the Mouse's Tank trailhead.

Route

From the Mouse's Tank parking lot, hike east down a sidewalk which quickly ends in a sandy wash. An easy, short sandy hike down-canyon takes you to Mouse's Tank. Keep your eyes open as there are numerous petroglyphs along the trail. Bypass Mouse's Tank on the left via a series of easy slabs and return back into the wash.

Continuing down-wash, the canyon temporarily narrows and a mandatory eight foot, class 4, downclimb will be required off a boulder. Keep in mind, this climb will be trickier on the return. Once the canyon widens, another dryfall will need to be bypassed which is easily accomplished on the left.

After 1.5 miles, when you're northwest of Crimson Staircase, look for a second wash that enters the main wash from the right. Hike 0.6 mile up this smaller wash until it terminates at the top of a small hill on the southwest side of the peak. Inspect the southwest face of Crimson Staircase for a prominent gully that leads to the summit. Navigate through a few sandstone fins to reach the base of this gully.

Climb up the gully where careful route finding is required to keep the scrambling class 3. A chimney blocks easy access to the top of the gully. Climb up the chimney, class 4, which will deposit you on a bench. Then hike 100 feet northwest to the base of the summit block. Don't be tempted to traverse on a bench west of the summit but instead scramble northeast up the southwest corner of the summit block to the top (class 3). The crimson red sandstone landscapes from the summit are sobering.

SOUTHWEST SLOPES VIA VOF HIGHWAY, CLASS 4

Distance: ~2.2 Miles
Elevation Gain: ~1,000 Feet

Time Required: 1.5-3 Hours
Rating: ★ ★ ★ ☆ ☆

Driving Directions

Drive 5.1 miles east on the Valley of Fire highway from the western entrance fee station or if you're driving from the eastern entrance, drive 1.9 miles west from the fee station and use a gravel pullout on the north side of the road. This is the trailhead.

Route

Although not as scenic as the Fire Canyon approach, this alternative is the fastest way to climb Crimson Staircase. This is not the most aesthetic way to climb this peak.

From the parking area, start hiking northwest up a wash. As the wash becomes harder to follow, hike north, then northeast through some red rock fins to the top of a hill on the southwest side of the peak. Inspect the southwest face of Crimson Staircase for a prominent gully that leads to the summit. Then navigate through a few sandstone fins to reach the base of this gully.

Climb up the gully where careful route finding is required to keep the scrambling class 3. A chimney blocks easy access to the top of the gully. Climb up the chimney, class 4, which will deposit you on a bench. Then hike 100 feet northwest to the base of the summit block. Don't be tempted to traverse on a bench west of the summit but instead scramble northeast up the southwest corner of the summit block to the top (class 3).

"Crimson Staircase" 2,454'
Southwest Slopes, Class 4

Class 4 Chimney

"Crimson Staircase" Map

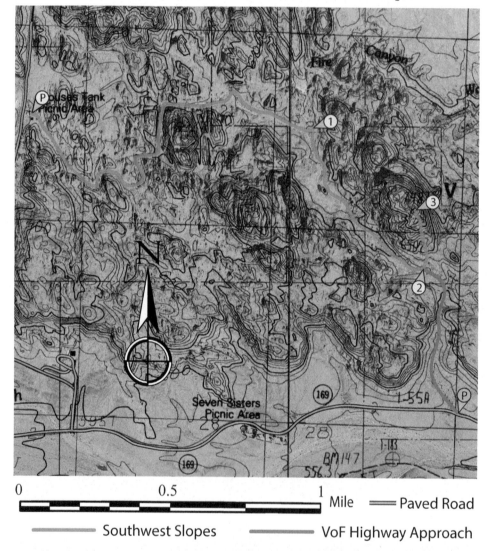

Key Waypoints	Latitude	Longitude
(P) Trailhead/Parking	N36.4410	W114.5161
(1) Wash Junction	N36.4404	W114.4995
(2) Top of Hill	N36.4340	W114.4930
(3) Summit	N36.4372	W114.4933
(P) VoF Highway Parking/TH	N36.4273	W114.4902

"FIRE HORN PEAK"   2,313'

Looking north from the Valley of Fire Highway, Fire Horn Peak is the most aesthetic-looking desert peak in the Park. Short and steep, this fine peak offers a quality scramble getting the most bang for the buck. This peak is also known as "The 5 Arch Peak" due to a unique arch located on the northwest side of the peak.

NORTH RIDGE, CLASS 4

Distance: ~1.5 Miles	Time Required: 1-2 Hours
Elevation Gain: ~800 Feet	Rating: ★ ★ ★ ★ ★

Driving Directions

Drive 6.3 miles east on the Valley of Fire highway from the west entrance fee station and turn left at a pullout for the Natural Arches/Charlie's Spring trailhead. If you're driving from the eastern entrance, drive 0.7 mile west from the fee station and turn right into the parking area. Do not block access to the service road.

Route

From the trailhead looking north, Fire Horn Peak appears to have six sub-summits. The true summit is the second summit from the left and has the most awe-striking, desert varnished summit horn. To reach the north ridge, locate a distinct rock gully, when viewed from the trailhead, in the middle of the six summits.

Begin by hiking up the Natural Arch trail for 300 yards. Look for a narrow wash on the right which exits from some astonishing cryptobiotic soil mounds. DO NOT hike up these dirt/mud mounds. Depart the Natural Arch trail, and follow the narrow wash as it meanders north towards the middle gully. Without climbing over the mounds, follow the wash directly as it deposits you directly at the base of the middle gully.

Scramble up the rocky gully to flatter terrain on the northeast side of the summit. Then hike to the base of the north ridge; the introduction is over.

Locate a steep slab, the only obvious path, which tops out in a wide chimney. Climb up the slab to a small bench (class 4). Continue left up a set of vertical cracks to gain the ridge proper (class 3) and then do a short exposed face climb with good features to the summit (class 3). Classic.

Nearing the summit on Fire Horn

Summit of Fire Horn. Photo by Tony Miles

"Fire Horn Peak" Map

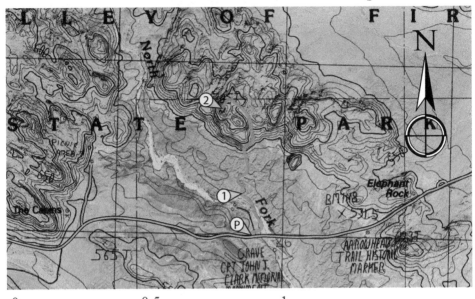

| 0 | 0.5 | 1 Mile | ═══ Paved Road |

Key Waypoints	Latitude	Longitude
P ▷ Parking/Trailhead	N36.4262	W114.4707
1 ▷ Leave Natural Arch Trail	N36.4282	W114.4712
2 ▷ Summit	N36.4328	W114.4728

"Fire Horn Peak" 2,313'
North Ridge, Class 4

Summit
Face Climb
Vertical Cracks
Class 4 Slab

"RED BARON"

2,312'

Despite being un-ranked, this peak is a worthy scrambling adventure. The views of Fire Canyon and surrounding peaks are jaw dropping. It's a good idea to have plenty of scrambling experience before attempting this peak since the summit boulder problem can be difficult. Exercise caution during the downclimb as this is a bad place to get hurt.

"Red Baron"

SOUTHEAST SLOPES, CLASS 5.3

Distance: ~3.0 Miles
Elevation Gain: ~800 Feet

Time Required: 1.5-2 Hours
Rating: ★ ★ ★ ★ ☆

Driving Directions

This trailhead is located outside of the eastern fee station. From the eastern fee station drive east 0.4 mile or if you're arriving from Overton, drive 1.6 miles from the beginning of the Valley of Fire highway from Northshore Road/Nevada 169 to a gravel pullout on the north side of the road. This is the trailhead. Do not start from the Elephant Rock parking area.

Route

Although much shorter, please do not start from the Elephant Rock parking area. There are areas of cryptobiotic soil which should be avoided. From the established pullout, carefully hike north avoiding any cryptobiotic soil to reach St. Thomas Wash.

Once in St. Thomas Wash, hike west until you are on the southeast side of the peak. When any junctions are encountered in the wash, stay on the northern (right) branch. Leave the wash, traverse around a small rock buttress and climb up a distinct gully located on the southeast side of the peak.

At the top of the gully, traverse around to the north side of the peak and look for a class 3 slab which leads to the summit block. There are two summit blocks and the western, harder-to-obtain summit is the correct summit.

Hike to the east side of the western summit block and find a heavily varnished desert face. It's the only reasonable way to the top. Carefully evaluate your footholds as they can be tricky to find on the descent. Fortunately the hard climbing is short lived and isn't very exposed. Climb up the varnished face, 5.3 for 15 feet, to the summit. The beginning moves of the boulder problem are the trickiest. As you climb upward, the climbing becomes easier but the rock quality diminishes.

Looking southwest from the top of "Red Baron".

"Red Baron Peak" & "Elephant Overlook" Map

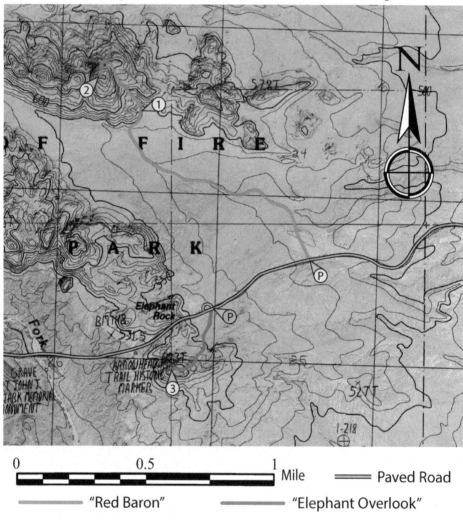

| | 0 | 0.5 | 1 Mile | ═══ Paved Road |

──── "Red Baron"   ──── "Elephant Overlook"

Key Waypoints	Latitude	Longitude
Ⓟ▷ Trailhead/Parking- "Red Baron"	N36.4315	W114.4510
①▷ Base of Southeast Gully	N36.4397	W114.4627
②▷ Summit of "Red Baron"	N36.4413	W114.4656
Ⓟ▷ Parking - "Elephant Overlook"	N36.4290	W114.4580
③▷ Summit of "Elephant Overlook"	N36.4255	W114.4606

"ELEPHANT OVERLOOK"   2,044'

When viewed from the west looking east, this peak appears to have a substantial prominence, towering over the southeastern side of the park. Elephant Overlook is a quick hike and the views are spectacular. For the most photogenic lighting, climb the peak in the morning hours.

EAST RIDGE, CLASS 2

Distance: ~0.7 Mile	Time Required: 30 Minutes-1 Hour
Elevation Gain: ~300 Feet	Rating: ★ ★ ☆ ☆ ☆

Driving Directions

This trailhead is the parking area for the Elephant Rock loop, located at the eastern fee station.

Route

From the eastern side of the Elephant Rock Parking area, cross the Valley of Fire highway and hike south up a wash to Elephant Overlook's east side. Do not be tempted to leave the wash early or start climbing up the northern aspect of the peak as there is a cliff that blocks easy access to the top. Follow the wash to Elephant Overlook's east ridge. Hike up the ridge, with some minor boulder hopping near the top, to the summit. The views to the west are astounding.

"NORTH FIRE PEAK" 3,743'

Anchoring the southern end of the park, North Fire Peak is the park's dominant peak. Reaching the summit from within the Valley of Fire is nearly impossible due to the imposing vertical north face cliffs that tower over the valley. The best route up this peak is from the Northshore Road/Nevada 169 in the Lake Mead National Recreation Area where a separate entrance fee of $20 (2016) is required. Expect a lot of off-trail hiking and go prepared with lots of water. This is a long hike.

EAST RIDGE, CLASS 2

Distance: ~8.8 Miles	Time Required: 4-7 Hours
Elevation Gain: ~2,800 Feet	Rating: ★ ★ ★ ☆ ☆

Driving Directions

Drive east through the Valley of Fire State Park until the Valley of Fire Highway ends at a "T" junction. Turn right (south) onto Northshore Road where you will quickly encounter the Lake Mead Recreation Area fee station. From the fee station, drive 5.7 miles south and make a right turn to the Rogers Spring picnic area. This is the trailhead.

Route

From the Rogers Spring parking area, follow the pavement to a bridge that crosses the headwaters of the spring. When the pavement ends, continue to hike up a distinct dirt trail as it meanders around some minor tributaries and slowly gains elevation.

When the trail ends or becomes hard to follow, start hiking west, northwest to the mouth of a large prominent limestone canyon. Work your way up the eastern slopes on the north side of this canyon. Careful route-finding is required to keep the hiking at class 2. These eastern slopes slowly transition into a long ridge that leads to the summit.

Once on the east ridge proper, enjoy fantastic views of the red sandstone peaks to the north and Lake Mead to the south. The east ridge snakes upward leading to a false summit, Northeast Fire. It's best to climb up and over Northeast Fire rather than to scramble down across a canyon leading to the true summit. Staying on the ridge between Northeast Fire and North Fire provides the easiest path to the top.

The north face dramatically drops off and the views of the park are stunning. Return the same way you came. And although shorter, don't be tempted to cut directly south back to Northshore Road. Complicated class 4 scrambling will be encountered.

Rogers Spring, Photo by Holly Gilhart Wolfe

"North Fire Peak" Map

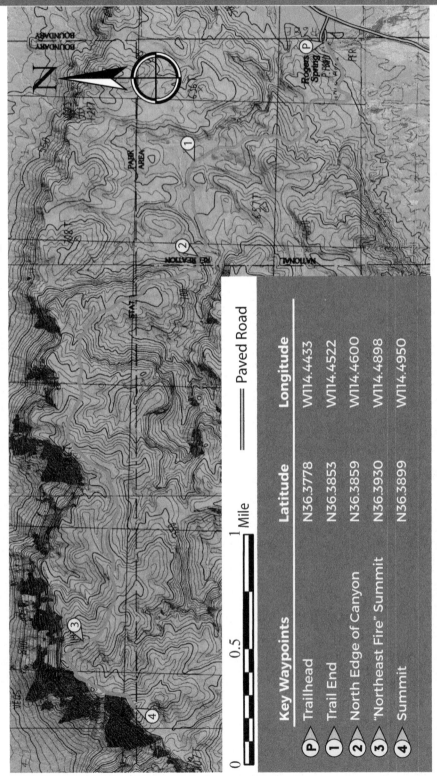

Key Waypoints	Latitude	Longitude
P ▷ Trailhead	N36.3778	W114.4433
1 ▷ Trail End	N36.3853	W114.4522
2 ▷ North Edge of Canyon	N36.3859	W114.4600
3 ▷ "Northeast Fire" Summit	N36.3930	W114.4898
4 ▷ Summit	N36.3899	W114.4950

Paved Road

0   0.5   1 Mile

Appendix A: Trail List

Trails are listed alphabetically

Name	Distance	Elevation Gain	Time Required	Rating	Page
Atlatl Rock	0.1 Mile	50 Feet	10-20 Minutes	Very Easy	Page 25
Balancing Rock	0.25 Mile	50 Feet	10-20 Minutes	Very Easy	Page 20
Charlie's Spring	4.8 Miles	300 Feet	2-4 Hours	Moderate	Page 30
Clark Memorial	0.2 Mile	50 Feet	15-30 Minutes	Very Easy	Page 30
Duck Rock	1.8 Miles	300 Feet	1-2 Hours	Easy	Page 39
Elephant Rock Loop	1.2 Miles	300 Feet	30 Minutes-1 Hour	Easy	Page 32
Fire Canyon	4.5 Miles	100-300 Feet	3-5 Hours	Very Difficult	Page 42
Fire Wash	2.6-5.2 Miles	50-300 Feet	1-2 Hours	Easy to Moderate	Page 40
Fire Wave	1.4 Miles	250 Feet	1-2 Hours	Easy	Page 14
Mouse's Tank	0.7 Mile	100 Feet	20-40 Minutes	Easy	Page 19
Natural Arches	2.5-5.2 Miles	100-300 Feet	1-4 Hours	Moderate	Page 28
Old Arrowhead Road	6.9-13.8 Miles	400-1,100 Feet	2.5-5 Hours	Moderate to Difficult	Page 33
Petrified Logs Loop West	0.3 Mile	50 Feet	10-20 Minutes	Very Easy	Page 24
Petrified Logs Loop East	0.1 Mile	50 Feet	10-20 Minutes	Very Easy	Page 24
Pinnacles Loop	4.8 Miles	500 Feet	2.5-4 Hours	Moderate	Page 22
Prospect Trail	4.8-9.6 Miles	600-900 Feet	2-5 Hours	Moderate to Difficult	Page 26
Rainbow Vista	1.1 Miles	150 Feet	30-45 Minutes	Easy	Page 16
White Domes Loop	1.1 Miles	300 Feet	30 Minutes-1.5 Hours	Easy	Page 14

Appendix B: Peak List

Sorted by Elevation

Rank	Name	Elevation	Prominence	Distance	Gain	Time Required	Rating	Page
1	"North Fire Peak"	3,743'	807'	8.8 Miles	2,800 Feet	4-7 Hours	★★★☆	Page 90
2	"Thin Peak"	3,694'	626'	1 Mile	700 Feet	30 Minutes-1 Hour	★★★☆	Page 62
3	Wesier Ridge South	3,077'	502'	3.2 Miles	700 Feet	1-2 Hours	★★☆☆	Page 47
4	"Duane Peak"	3,002'	689'	5.6 Miles	1,200 Feet	2.5-4 Hours	★☆☆☆	Page 65
5	"Gregg Peak"	2,999'	358'	4.2 Miles	800 Feet	2-3 Hours	★☆☆☆	Page 63
6	"Valley Of Fire Peak"	2,972'	626'	4.4-5.6 Miles	1,200-1,400 Feet	3-5 Hours	★★★★	Page 69
7	"Weekapaug Mountain"	2,674'	328'	1.4 Miles	700 Feet	1-2 Hours	★★★☆	Page 67
8	"Cairn Peak"	2,497'	381'	0.9 Mile	400 Feet	30-45 Minutes	★★☆☆	Page 74
9	"Crimson Staircase"	2,454'	436'	2.2-5.1 Miles	1,000-1,100 Feet	1.5-4 Hours	★★★★	Page 80
10	Point 2,431	2,431'	315'	3 Miles	500 Feet	1.5-2 Hours	★★★☆	Page 55
11	Baseline Mesa	2,378'	361'	3.8 Miles	800 Feet	2-3 Hours	★★☆☆	Page 77
	Silica Dome	2,349'	233'	1 Mile	250 Feet	30-45 Minutes	★★★☆	Page 76
12	"Fire Horn Peak"	2,313'	427'	1.5 Miles	800 Feet	1-2 Hours	★★★★	Page 83
S	"Boneyard Peak"	2,312'	295'	3.4 Miles	600 Feet	1.5-2 Hours	★★★★	Page 57
S	"Red Baron"	2,312'	295'	3 Miles	800 Feet	1.5-2 Hours	★★★☆	Page 86
13	"The Orphan"	2,280'	328'	3.2 Miles	500 Feet	1.5-2 Hours	★★★★	Page 58
14	"Sitting Monkey"	2,260'	324'	2.9 Miles	700 Feet	2-3 Hours	★★★☆	Page 48
	East White Dome	2,234'	282'	0.4 Mile	250 Feet	20-40 Minutes	★★★☆	Page 53

Rank	Name	Elevation	Prominence	Distance	Gain	Time Required	Rating	Page
	Gibraltar Rock	2,171'	187'	1.6 Miles	450 Feet	1-2 Hours	★★★☆	Page 51
	West White Dome	2,116'	99'	0.3 Mile	100 Feet	15-30 Minutes	★★★☆	Page 52
	"Elephant Overlook"	2,044'	207'	0.7 Mile	300 Feet	30 Minutes-1 Hour	★★☆☆	Page 89

Notes:

· A ranked peak is a peak that has more than 300 feet of prominence.

· Prominence is defined as the measure of summit height minus the saddle height – the low point of the highest connecting summit to an elevation greater than the peaks' elevation.

· Peaks listed with "S" are considered soft ranked but could potentially qualify as ranked. The lack of saddle/summit elevations listed on USGS maps along with not interpolating elevations, could qualify these peaks as ranked.

· Names in quotes are considered unofficial.

· List was compiled with the help of John Kirk and sourced from www.listsofjohn.com.

Acknowledgments

I would like to thank my wife, Donna, for her tremendous patience in dealing with my obsession of the outdoors. Her support and encouragement has been of uttermost importance in helping me complete this book.

A special thanks goes to the staff at the Valley of Fire State Park for their help.

Thanks to Courtney Purcell, David Goldstein and John Kirk for additional information on the peaks.

Also, thanks to all of my partners who helped me run and hike the trails along with helping me climb the peaks. This includes: Mandy Eskelson, Gerod Green, Tony Miles and Holly Gilhart Wolfe.

Finally, thanks to anyone I may have left out that joined me along the way.

About the Author

Derek Wolfe spends as much time as possible enjoying the adventure lifestyle presented by the Rocky Mountains of Colorado, high desert wilderness of Utah, and Mojave Desert of Nevada. An enthusiastic (some might argue obsessive) mountaineer and rock climber, he has climbed all 637 mountains higher than 13,000' in Colorado. Additionally, he participates in cave exploration and mapping in the region's caves as well as those in Tennessee, New Mexico and South Dakota.

Channeling one of his muses, Edward Abbey, he has produced this guide in an effort to educate and enlighten those fellow adventure seekers who venture into the magnificent desert environment. His goal is to encourage those who use this guidebook to learn and practice proper minimalist impact techniques so that these magnificent lands can be enjoyed by future generations.